Improving Research through User Engagement

There are increasing calls for social science researchers to work more closely with research users. References to engaging users in and with research are now common in research funding requirements, national research strategies and large-scale research programmes. User engagement has therefore become part of the rhetoric of educational and social science research. But what is user engagement, how can it be achieved and what challenges and opportunities does it present for researchers and research users?

The authors of this new book present an authoritative overview of recent theoretical debates, practical developments and empirical evidence on the role of user engagement in contemporary educational and social science research. The book focuses on the relationship between user engagement and research design, and emphasizes how user engagement needs to be understood as an interplay between the different kinds of knowledge and expertise held by researchers and users. Drawing on evidence from studies involving different kinds of research users, there is detailed discussion of the dynamics and complexities of working with practitioners, service users and policy-makers. The authors make clear that user engagement has definite implications for the way in which research is designed, managed and commissioned, and the way in which researchers and research users are trained, supported and encouraged to interact.

Written for the many professionals involved in funding, doing and using research within education and other social sciences, this book provides:

- conceptual guidance on different approaches and interpretations of user engagement

- examples and evidence of effective strategies for engaging practitioners, service users and policy-makers
- capacity-building ideas and implications for researchers and research users
- specific suggestions as to how the conceptualization, management, scaling up and evidence base of user engagement could be improved.

At the core of this forward-thinking text is a robust analysis of an important facet of modern social science research. The authors' evidence-based, evaluative approach provides a useful, detailed analysis of an area of social science research methodology that is increasingly valued and emphasized by research councils and mediators.

Mark Rickinson is an independent educational researcher and a Research Fellow in the Department of Education at the University of Oxford, UK.

Judy Sebba is Professor of Education and Director of Research and Knowledge Exchange in the School of Education and Social Work at the University of Sussex, UK.

Anne Edwards is a Professor and Director of the Department of Education at the University of Oxford, UK.

Improving Learning TLRP

Series Editor: Andrew Pollard, Director of the ESRC Teaching and Learning Programme

The Improving Learning series showcases findings from projects within ESRC's Teaching and Learning Research Programme (TLRP) – the UK's largest ever coordinated educational research initiative. Each book is explicitly designed to support 'evidence-informed' decisions in educational practice and policy-making. In particular, they combine rigorous social and educational science with high awareness of the significance of the issues being researched.

Improving Mathematics at Work
Edited by Celia Hoyles, Richard Noss, Phillip Kent and Arthur Bakker

Improving the Context for Inclusion
Andy Howes, S.M.B. Davies and Sam Fox

Improving Working as Learning
Alan Felstead, Alison Fuller, Nick Jewson and Lorna Unwin

Improving Literacy by Teaching Morphemes
Terezinha Nunes and Peter Bryant

Improving Workplace Learning
Karen Evans, Phil Hodkinson, Helen Rainbird and Lorna Unwin

Improving Schools, Developing Inclusion
Mel Ainscow, Tony Booth and Alan Dyson

Improving Subject Teaching
Robin Millar, John Leach, Jonathan Osborne and Mary Ratcliffe

Improving Learning Cultures in Further Education
David James and Gert Biesta

Improving Learning How to Learn
Mary James, Robert McCormick, Paul Black, Patrick Carmichael, Mary-Jane Drummond, Alison Fox, John MacBeath, Bethan Marshall, David Pedder, Richard Procter, Sue Swaffield, Joanna Swann and Dylan Wiliam

Improving Learning through Consulting Pupils
Jean Rudduck and Donald McIntyre

Improving Learning, Skills and Inclusion
Frank Coffield, Sheila Edward, Ian Finlay, Ann Hodgson, Ken Spours and Richard Steer

Improving Classroom Learning with ICT
Rosamund Sutherland

Improving Learning in College
Roz Ivanic, Richard Edwards, David Barton, Marilyn Martin-Jones, Zoe Fowler, Buddug Hughes, Greg Mannion, Kate Miller, Candice Satchwell and June Smith

Improving Learning in Later Life
Alexandra Withnall

Improving Learning by Widening Participation in Higher Education
Edited by Miriam David

Improving Research through User Engagement
Mark Rickinson, Judy Sebba and Anne Edwards

Improving What is Learned at University
John Brennan

Improving Inter-professional Collaborations
Anne Edwards, Harry Daniels, Tony Gallagher, Jane Leadbetter and Paul Warmington

Improving Learning in a Professional Context
Edited by Jim McNally and Allan Blake

Improving Disabled Students' Learning
Mary Fuller, Jan Georgeson, Mick Healey, Alan Hurst, Katie Kelly, Sheila Riddell, Hazel Roberts and Elizabet Weedon

Improving Research through User Engagement

Mark Rickinson, Judy Sebba and Anne Edwards

Routledge
Taylor & Francis Group

LONDON AND NEW YORK

First edition published 2011
by Routledge
2 Park Square, Milton Park, Abingdon, Oxon, OX14 4RN

Simultaneously published in the USA and Canada
by Routledge
270 Madison Avenue, New York, NY 10016

*Routledge is an imprint of the Taylor & Francis Group, an informa
business*

Typeset in Charter ITC and Stone Sans by
Pindar NZ, Auckland, New Zealand
Printed and bound in Great Britain by
TJ International Ltd, Padstow, Cornwall

British Library Cataloguing in Publication Data
A catalogue record for this book is available from the British
Library

Library of Congress Cataloging-in-Publication Data
 Rickinson, Mark.
 Improving research through user engagement / Mark
Rickinson, Judy Sebba, and Anne Edwards. — 1st ed.
 p. cm.
 Includes bibliographical references and index.
 1. Social sciences—Research. 2. Education—Research. I. Sebba,
Judy. II. Edwards, Anne, 1946- III. Title.
 H62.R476 2011
 001.4'2—dc22   2010035445

ISBN13: 978-0-415-46168-9 (hbk)
ISBN13: 978-0-415-46169-6 (pbk)
ISBN13: 978-0-203-83130-4 (ebk)

*In memory of Jean Rudduck
and Donald McIntyre who led the way*

Contents

Illustrations

Boxes

Figures

Table

Preface

The Improving Learning series showcases findings from projects within ESRC's Teaching and Learning Research Programme (TLRP) – the UK's largest ever coordinated educational research initiative.

Books in the Improving Learning series are explicitly designed to support 'evidence-informed' decisions in educational practice and policy-making. In particular, they combine rigorous social and educational science with high awareness of the significance of the issue being researched.

Working closely with practitioners, organizations and agencies covering all educational sectors, the programme has supported many of the UK's best researchers to work on the direct improvement of policy and practice to support learning. Over 60 projects have been supported, covering many issues across the lifecourse. We are proud to present the results of this work through books in the Improving Learning series.

Each book provides a concise, accessible and definitive overview of innovative findings from TLRP investment. If more advanced information is required, the books may be used as a gateway to academic journals, monographs, websites, etc. Alternatively, shorter summaries and research briefings on key findings are also available via the programme's website at www.tlrp.org.

We hope that you will find the analysis and findings presented in this book are helpful to you in your work on improving outcomes for learners.

Andrew Pollard
Director, Teaching and Learning Research Programme
Institute of Education, University of London

Acknowledgements

We are grateful to the many colleagues and friends who contributed to this book, in particular through the ESRC-funded Thematic Seminar Series 'Making a Difference: Working with Users to Develop Educational Research' during 2005 and 2006. Three groups of people contributed – the seminar presenters, the seminar participants and the core planning group – who met between seminars to move us forward in our thinking and identify the next steps. Membership of these groups overlapped but we have listed each person only once while acknowledging that some contributed in all three ways. The affiliations listed are those that applied at the time of the seminars. In addition, special thanks go to Gill Boag-Munroe for proofreading the final manuscript. Finally, we are grateful to the following organizations and authors for granting us permission to reproduce published tables and diagrams within this book: the Social Care Institute for Excellence (Box 3.1), CfBT Education Trust (Box 3.2), and Professor Sandra Nutley (Figure 5.1).

Core planning group

Gary Brace, General Teaching Council for Wales
Alan Brown, University of Warwick
Philippa Cordingley, Centre for the Use of Research and Evidence in Education
Alan Dyson, The University of Manchester
Richard Edwards, University of Sterling
John Gardner, Queen's University Belfast
Ann Lewis, University of Birmingham
Joan Lloyd, University of Birmingham
Donald McIntyre, University of Cambridge

Pamela Munn, The University of Edinburgh
Tim Oates, Qualifications and Curriculum Agency
Gareth Rees, Cardiff University and Research Capacity Building
    Network
Chris Robertson, University of Birmingham
Lesley Saunders, General Teaching Council for England
Felicity Wikeley, University of Bath
Jill Wilson, National Teacher Research Panel

Seminar presenters

Marion Barnes, University of Brighton
Philip Barker, City of Bristol College
Richard Bartholomew, Department for Education and Skills
Tom Bentley, Demos
Robin Bevan, King Edward VI Grammar School, Chelmsford
Janet Brewer, City of Bristol College
Donald Christie, University of Strathclyde, Glasgow
Phil Davies, Government Social Research Unit
Peter Dudley, National College for School Leadership
Sue Duncan, Government Chief Social Researcher
Danny Durant, Worcestershire County Council
Brian Fender, previously Higher Education Funding Council for
    England and Funders' Forum
Graham Handscomb, Essex County Council
Andrew Hunt, Nuffield Curriculum Centre
Mary James, Institute of Education, University of London, London
    and Teaching and Learning Research Programme
David Leat, Newcastle University
Robin Millar, The University of York
Sandra Nutley, University of St Andrews
Andrew Pollard, Institute of Education, University of London,
    London and Teaching and Learning Research Programme
Michael Preston-Shoot, University of Bedfordshire
Catrin Roberts, Nuffield Foundation
John Samuels, previously Hampshire County Council

Seminar participants

Apostolov Apostol, University of Oxford
David Budge, previously *Times Educational Supplement*

Donald Evans, Centre for the Use of Research and Evidence in
    Education
Els De Geest, University of Oxford
John Harris, Barnardos
Roz Ivanič, Lancaster University
Peter John, University of Plymouth
Jane Lowe, Lauder College, Dunfermline
Andrew Morris, National Educational Research Forum
Federica Olivero, University of Bristol
Katherine Pinnock, University of Birmingham
Esther Saville, Scottish Executive
Caroline Sharp, National Foundation for Educational Research
Christine Skelton, Roehampton University
Amanda Williams, Economic and Social Research Council
Martin Young, Cranford Park Primary School, Hayes

PART I
WHAT IS THE ISSUE?

Chapter 1

Introduction

In this opening chapter, we introduce user engagement as integral to current efforts aimed at improving the generation, mediation and utilization of research-based knowledge across the social sciences and public policy. We outline our perspective on user engagement in terms of an interplay of the different kinds of knowledge and expertise held by researchers and users. We then consider its connection with debates and developments concerning: research quality and relevance, modes of knowledge production, and research use and impact. We argue that user engagement needs to be understood as a complex and problematic concept that can present challenges and tensions for researchers and research users alike. This is illustrated through four key areas of potential difficulty: conceptualization, manageability, superficiality and limitations in scale, and evidence base. The chapter ends with an overview of the structure of the rest of the book.

Background

User engagement has become part of the landscape of contemporary social science research. Against the backdrop of evidence-based policy and practice agendas as well as critical questioning of much social science research, calls for increased involvement of research users in and with research have proliferated. References to user engagement are now seen in research funding requirements, national research strategies, international policy developments and a growing number of practical initiatives. All applications to the UK's Economic and Social Research Council (ESRC), for example, must specify plans for 'Communication and User Engagement', and 'being of value to potential users' is held up as one of the five characteristics of all successful ESRC research applications (ESRC 2009b: 9). Similarly, charitable funders such as the Nuffield

Foundation make it clear that applicants should 'have identified those to whom the outcomes of the project will be most relevant, and have engaged them where possible from the early stages' (Nuffield Foundation 2010: 2).

More and more large-scale strategic research developments have at their centre notions of partnership, collaboration and engagement. The UK Teaching and Learning Research Programme (TLRP) explicitly emphasized 'user engagement throughout the research process', both in terms of practitioner involvement in projects and liaison with national user and policy organizations (Pollard 2004: 17). Similarly, the Scottish Applied Educational Research Scheme (AERS) was based on the core principle that 'the best way to enhance the infrastructure of educational research is through collaboration and a spirit of inclusiveness' (Munn *et al.* 2003: 4). Alongside these developments, there are also increasing numbers of research projects, programmes and centres seeking strong user representation on advisory panels and steering groups, and growing interest in collaborative and participative approaches within primary research and research synthesis. In this way, user engagement has become integral to efforts aimed at reforming and improving knowledge generation, mediation and utilization across many areas of public policy.

Despite these developments, it is our contention that user engagement remains poorly understood both as a concept and as a process. In this book, we look at users in terms of practitioners (those involved in guiding learning, shaping learning environments and supporting learners' well-being), service users (children, young people, adults, families and/or identified groups receiving specialized services), and policy-makers (local, regional and national politicians, civil servants and administrators, political advisors, research funders and government agencies staff). Some users in each of these groups will have specific research skills such as basic inquiry skills that they learned during school and/or in further and higher education. Some may have significant expertise and experience on which to draw when either using or engaging in research. We look at the engagement of users both in terms of being involved in research processes (engagement *in* research) and engagement with research outputs (engagement *with* research). Most importantly, we see user engagement in terms of an interplay between the different kinds of knowledge and expertise held by researchers and different users. Hence, we explore user engagement in terms of knowledge exchange processes that involve different players, are multi-directional and have strong personal and affective dimensions.

Taking this view, we see the task of involving users in and with research as a demanding undertaking that asks new questions of research and necessitates new skills from researchers and research users alike. Furthermore, as shown by reviews of strategic initiatives such as TLRP, we are aware that user engagement can raise difficult political and ethical questions:

> The risk of tokenistic forms of engagement, the competing pressures on users' time and capacity to engage, the particular kinds of skills and understandings that this kind of work requires of researchers, as well as deeper-seated issues relating to the politics of user engagement, user roles and research ownership, were manifest to different degrees across the Programme.
>
> (Rickinson *et al.* 2005: 21)

In view of these complexities, this book draws together recent theoretical debates, practical developments and empirical evidence on how research might be developed through user engagement. It seeks to provide:

* conceptual guidance on different approaches and interpretations of user engagement;
* examples and evidence of effective strategies for engaging practitioners, service users and policy-makers;
* capacity-building ideas and implications for researchers and research users.

The arguments and examples presented in this book grew out of a TLRP-funded thematic seminar series which, in 2005 and 2006, explored the implications of different forms of user engagement for the design of educational research (see Appendix). Seminar participants included researchers from TLRP projects, senior civil servants, representatives of research funding organizations, education practitioners, research mediators, government analysts and policy advisors, and researchers from fields beyond education such as social work and health.

One of the most important things that became clear during the seminar series was the dynamic nature of the terrain and debates surrounding user engagement. It was clear that initiatives such as TLRP and AERS have afforded researchers the opportunity to try out various strategies and approaches to working with users. Practical knowledge and reflective understanding on this issue is therefore developing. At the same time, the landscape of knowledge generation, mediation and utilization right across public policy has been fast changing as new players, practices and processes have taken shape. It is therefore crucial that our discussions of user engagement are set within the context of wider developments in social research, policy and practice. It is also critical that user engagement is approached as a complex and problematic concept in its own right with inherent challenges and tensions. It is to these two issues of wider contexts and challenges, and tensions, that we now turn in the following two sections.

Contexts and dimensions of user engagement

While interest in researcher–user collaboration and knowledge utilization is by no means new (e.g. Weiss 1979; Huberman 1987, 1990), contemporary support for user engagement needs to be understood within the context of recent developments in social science research and public policy generally. As shown in Figure 1.1, user engagement has close connections with strategies and debates concerning research quality and relevance, knowledge generation, and research use and impact. These concerns, in turn, can be linked with wider social trends relating to user-led services, the knowledge economy and public services accountability.

Improving research relevance and quality

A common argument within critiques of social science research has been that it has been too 'supplier-driven' and so insufficiently focused on issues of importance to users (in education, for example, see Hillage *et al.* 1998; Prost 2001). Alongside relevance, there have also been concerns about quality. Reviews of educational research in England, for instance, argued that where research did address policy and practice questions, it tended to be small scale, insufficiently based on existing knowledge and presented in a way that was largely inaccessible to non-academic audiences (Hillage *et al.* 1998).

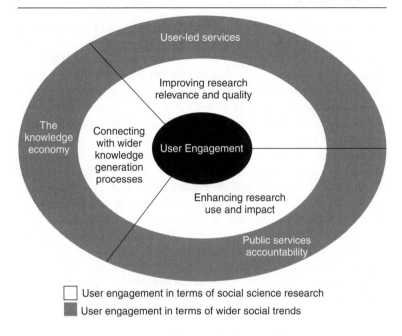

Figure 1.1 User engagement developments in research and wider society

Greater involvement of, and collaboration with, research users has been seen as an important way to redress such shortcomings (Rudduck and McIntyre 1998). This thinking can be seen very clearly in the policies and publications of major funders. The ESRC, for example, emphasizes that 'on-going relationships between researchers and research users are the key to ensuring that research is relevant and timely' (ESRC 2009a: 15). Along similar lines, leaders within the educational research community have argued that:

> [t]o be convincing, to claim authority, we have to demonstrate both the relevance and the quality of our work. [. . .] This is the rationale for the authentic engagement of research users at every stage of the research process, from the conceptualization of key research issues onwards.
>
> (Pollard 2004: 17)

The contribution of users to research agendas is an important part of the potential link between user engagement and research relevance. With this, however, there is the very important question of scale and the need for partnerships with research users to be strategic as well as project-based. As Hargreaves (1998: 128) has argued: 'Users must play a role in shaping the direction of educational research as a whole, not just in influencing a local project in which they happen to be involved'.

Thus, approaches to user engagement are intricately bound up with efforts at many levels to improve the quality and relevance of social science research. This is important because it helps to explain why user engagement can raise concerns about political influence amongst some researchers, how discussions of user engagement need to be sensitive to research genres and their different conceptions of knowledge; and how issues of scale (local versus national, individual versus institutional) cannot be overlooked. It also underlines the way in which research is part of broader change processes happening across public services: namely, increasing emphasis on user-led and personalized services based on the vision of 'giving people who use services power over what they use [as] part of a general trend towards providing services that prioritize independent living, choice and inclusion' (Bartlett 2009: 7).

Connecting with wider knowledge production

Another important context for user engagement is the evolution of ideas about knowledge generation within democratic societies. It has been clear for some years that the nature of knowledge production is changing in many areas of science, technology and social science. As Gibbons *et al.* (1994: 19) argued in the early 1990s:

> A new form of knowledge production is emerging alongside the traditional, familiar one [. . .]. These changes are described in terms of a shift in emphasis from a Mode 1 to a Mode 2. Mode 1 is discipline-based and carries a distinction between what is fundamental and what is applied [. . .]. By contrast, Mode 2 knowledge production is transdisiplinary. It is characterized by constant flow back and forth between the fundamental and the applied, between the theoretical and the practical. Typically, discovery occurs in contexts where knowledge is developed [. . .] and put to use.

While these ideas were developed largely in the context of science and technology, their ramifications for knowledge production within social sciences such as education have not gone unnoticed. Publications on educational research, for example, have argued that Gibbons *et al.*'s work 'alerts us to the fact that research and researchers are not the universal sources of knowledge' (Hodkinson and Smith 2004: 155) and 'gives us an idea of how research and practice can inform each other and support each other' (Furlong and Oancea 2005: 8). The underlying point is that developments such as user engagement cannot be isolated from the fact that 'the contexts of knowledge production and use in society are diversifying and new models of research are being developed to respond to these challenges' (Furlong and Oancea 2005: 6).

User engagement needs to be understood not just as a way of addressing concerns about quality and relevance, but also as a way of academic research learning from the many other modes and forms of knowledge generation and mediation going on beyond the academy. In this way, user engagement raises interesting and important questions about research design, project leadership and researcher and user capacity building. As will become clear in later chapters, the varying time scales and priorities of different players involved in the research process can present considerable challenges for project management. Project management thus becomes the weaving together of different forms of expertise, priorities and time scales across a variety of sites. This, like other aspects of user engagement, has significant capacity-building implications for researchers, users and mediators.

Enhancing research use and impact

Alongside issues of research quality and knowledge generation, user engagement also needs to be seen as closely connected with questions of research use and impact. The last 15 years have seen significant changes in the expectations and demands placed upon social research. The growth of evidence-based or evidence-informed policy movements internationally, coupled with concerns over the accountability of public services expenditures, have increasingly put the spotlight on issues of research impact and research utilization. As a report on the topic from the ESRC describes:

In parallel with the ESRC's continuing commitment to impact assessment, the Government in recent years has also placed increasing emphasis on the need to provide evidence of the economic and social returns from its investment in research. This trend was reinforced in the Warry report [. . .] to the (then) DTI in 2006, which recommended that the Research Councils 'should make strenuous efforts to demonstrate more clearly the impact they already achieve from their investments'.

(ESRC 2009a: 2)

Such imperatives have, of course, played out very obviously in national systems for the assessment of research quality. Within the UK, for example, the new Research Excellence Framework is anticipated to place a higher value on scholarly and practical impacts rather than just focusing on research outputs. The intention is that '[s]ignificant additional recognition will be given where researchers build on excellent research to deliver demonstrable benefits to the economy, society, public policy, culture and quality of life' (HEFCE 2009). There are also proposals for 'a substantive input into the assessment of impact by representatives of the users, beneficiaries and wider audiences of research' (HEFCE 2010: 3). The challenges of measuring impact have been acknowledged for many years, with McIntyre (1998: 196) suggesting that 'whether or not it is possible, it is certainly necessary'.

As well as these very real changes in the material conditions of social science research, there have also been important conceptual developments within the social sciences in terms of understandings of research impact and use. Put simply, research use has moved from being a largely peripheral concern to become 'a very significant practical and intellectual challenge' (Nutley *et al.* 2007: 3). The utilization of research and evidence in policy and practice settings has emerged as a legitimate topic for theoretical and empirical inquiry. Understandings of the processes and factors involved have become more diverse and nuanced. More linear ideas of research dissemination and knowledge transfer have been challenged by more complex notions of research utilization and knowledge mediation, brokerage and translation. As the authors of a recent paper entitled 'Why "knowledge transfer" is misconceived for applied social research' argue:

Research on how research outputs inform understanding and get used suggest that use is best characterized as a continual and iterative process, one that draws on diverse kinds of knowledge through many different channels and routes and involves more or less translation or indeed transformation along the way. Interpersonal and social interactions are often seen as key to accessing and interpreting such research knowledge, whether among policy or practice colleagues, research intermediaries or more directly with researchers themselves.

(Davies *et al.* 2008: 189)

Seen from this kind of perspective, the potential connection between concerns about research impact and processes of user engagement are very clear. The ESRC is not alone amongst funders in delineating 'the key factors that are vital for impact generation' as:

- established relationships and networks with user communities
- involving users at all stages of the research
- well-planned user engagement and knowledge exchange strategies
- portfolios of research activity that build reputations with research users
- good infrastructure and management support
- where appropriate, the involvement of intermediaries and knowledge brokers as translators, amplifiers, network providers.

(ESRC 2009a: 14)

Achieving all or even some of the above, however, takes time, resources, effort, relationships, systems and skills. Here again, then, user engagement can be seen to raise conceptual and practical questions about understanding and negotiating knowledge and expertise, as well as political questions concerning the role and expectations of research in society. This brings us to the challenges and tensions associated with user engagement.

Challenges and tensions of user engagement

As noted earlier, the concept of user engagement has not been without criticism and the process of seeking to engage users in and with research has not been without difficulties. Based on discussions during the seminar series as well as accounts in the wider literature, we see four key areas of challenge and critique. These concern user engagement being:

- poorly conceptualized
- difficult to manage
- superficial or limited in scale
- weakly evidenced.

Conceptualization

One criticism of user engagement is that lack of conceptual clarity about its nature and purposes have hampered its development in practice and theory. This was flagged up clearly by the mid-term review of TLRP, which reported that

> [a] view held by some researchers was that progress . . . . had been held up by a lack of clear thinking about the notion of user engagement. One interviewee saw the focus on user engage-ment as an insufficiently thought-through 'response to being beaten by the public discourse about educational research'. This individual argued that it was all too easy for user engagement to be seen as an easy panacea for improving the relevance of educational research.
>
> (Rickinson *et al.* 2005: 16)

The next chapter looks in more detail at the conceptualization of user engagement, but there are two common stumbling blocks that are worth highlighting here. The first concerns the fact that research users comprise 'multiple, overlapping publics whose boundaries and characteristics are ill-defined' (Foster and Hammersley 1998: 613). Quite different user engagement approaches can therefore be required for different kinds of policy-makers (e.g. politicians versus political advisors versus government analysts), practitioners (e.g. school leaders versus classroom teachers versus social workers) and service users (e.g. students versus parents versus special interest groups). Furthermore, any formulation of engagement strategies must also take into account the growing number of research media-tors and brokers operating on the boundaries and intersections of policy, practice and research. The growing significance of various kinds of 'go-betweens', 'mediators' and 'brokerage agencies' is a common finding from many recent analyses of public policy processes (e.g. Saunders 2007a; OECD/CERI 2007) and a theme we will return to throughout the book.

A second source of conceptual difficulty is where user engagement strategies are limited by simplistic conceptions of the research engagement process. It is now well established that understandings of how users engage with and use research have been unhelpfully straightforward:

> [While] much attention has been focused on instrumental use of research – where research evidence has concrete and visible impact on the action and choices of policy-makers and practitioners [. . .] [w]e know that, on the ground, research is often used in more subtle, indirect and conceptual ways [. . .] altering the ways in which policy makers and practitioners think about what they do, how they do it and why.
>
> (Nutley *et al.* 2007: 301)

Views of research engagement have also tended to underplay the social and interactive nature of the process and therefore overlook the 'two-way rather than unilinear flows of knowledge, in which researchers and research users each bring their own experience, values and understanding to bear in interpreting research and its meaning for local contexts' (Nutley *et al.* 2007: 305).

Manageability

A second issue is that enabling effective user engagement presents very real demands for research teams and research leaders. A number of contributors to the seminar series emphasized the time (and therefore additional resource) that is required to negotiate and sustain ongoing engagement processes with practitioner and policy colleagues. This is echoed by recent evaluations of collaborative research ventures such as AERS in Scotland where it was noted that

> collaborative research activity is likely to incur higher costs than other more traditional research, since it is generally less efficient on the resources available.
>
> (Taylor *et al.* 2007: 15)

As well as time and resources, collaboration and engagement also require new kinds of skills and capabilities amongst researchers. These skills are associated much more with 'know who' as opposed to 'know what and know how' (Lundvall 1996: 8), and concerned with managing relationships and weaving together different forms of expertise and priorities during the research process.

As well as being demanding for researchers, user engagement can also present challenges for research users. A literature review that adopted a collaborative approach with educational practitioners and researchers analysing published research noted that

> [t]he responses of the group [of practitioners] indicated that they were feeling their way with the methodology, often with a sense of isolation and faltering confidence both in themselves and in the systematic process. There was a strong feeling [. . .] that considerable time had been needed to develop an understanding of the approach.
>
> (Kahn *et al.* 2006: 9)

Furthermore, the challenge of getting to grips with the conceptual demands of the project's substantive tasks was not helped by the fact that 'the process of engaging with the project was an additional burden on top of the normal workload [and] not necessarily seen (by themselves or others) as a priority in their use of time' (Kahn *et al.* 2006: 9). Very similar kinds of issues were identified with respect to the involvement of practitioner partners in some TLRP projects due to various factors ranging from 'time pressures on attending meetings or undertaking project activities through to deeper-seated structural constraints on particular ways of thinking and working' (Rickinson *et al.* 2005: 16).

Superficiality and limitations in scale

As well as being difficult to manage, a further difficulty associated with user engagement is that it is easy to address in limited or superficial ways. Concerns have been raised, for example, about research proposals including details about user engagement simply because it is a requirement for funding. Writing in the late 1990s, Hargreaves (1998: 128) talked about the 'danger of researchers playing at user involvement in a superficial or rhetorical way because the rules of the "game" of obtaining funding and doing research have not really changed'. A similar point was made by a practitioner involved in the TLRP commissioning process felt that 'it was difficult to know if what was written [in project proposals] was just a nod towards user engagement because people had to put something in' (Rickinson *et al.* 2005: 15).

Another limitation is where user involvement is restricted to certain less-important parts of the research process. An example from educational research might be school or college-based practitioners playing a role in collecting data and/or communicating recommendations but not in formulating research questions or analysing data. There can also be limitations in terms of level (individual as opposed to organization) and scale (local as opposed to system). Nutley *et al.*'s (2007: 302) analysis of research use in public policy highlights 'a tendency in the literature to treat research use as a primarily individualized process'. There are similar risks with user engagement: namely, an over emphasis on the engagement of small numbers of individual users during the research process with little thought given to the engagement of larger networks of institutions during and after the research process. Indeed, a recent study in Canada has confirmed that 'the majority of efforts aimed at enhancing research utilization are focused at the level of the research project, research unit or research discipline. [. . .] Few academic institutions have developed an institution-wide capacity to support research–research user collaboration' (Phipps and Shapson 2009: 214).

A major challenge for establishing widespread user engagement in research relates to the difficulties of 'scaling up' such approaches so that they become the norm rather than the exception. Funders have assisted in this by extending their requirements for researchers to address user engagement. This top-down approach needs to be matched by bottom-up approaches such as creating networks between single researchers and individual institutions engaging with users. Examples of this are given in later chapters. The hope is that this will contribute towards 'systemic' change in how research is conceived, implemented, reported and subsequently used.

Evidence base

Finally, some critics of user engagement have argued that it is an idea whose benefits are not well evidenced. For example, in a paper about the co-production of knowledge between management academics and practitioners, Knight and Pettigrew (2007: 1) report 'few articles based on primary data [. . .] despite considerable and growing interest in the subject'. Nutley *et al.* (2007: 2) note a similar point about the empirical underpinnings of evidence-based approaches generally: 'The irony here is that the evidence base confirming any benefits (or indeed, dysfunctions) of an evidence-based approach to public policy and service delivery is actually rather thin. ' These latter authors do stress, however, that 'an absence of evidence' should not be confused with 'an evidence of absence' (3). That said, in the case of user engagement, there does seem to be a lot more rhetorical writing about its potential benefits than empirical inquiry into its processes and impacts. Studies of research impact are an important exception to this since they have often flagged up researcher–user interactions and relationships as a key contributor to impact. Three examples from analyses of social science research are given below:

> In all the impact case studies, the most important factor contributing to the generation of impact was *the pre-existence of networks and relationships with research users.* Sustained contacts with users, based on personal relationships and built up over the long term were the most important channels for policy and practice applications. [emphasis added]
>
> (ESRC 2009a: 14)

> When *researchers remain active in the setting over time, and negotiate their presence carefully,* we are likely to get an upward shift in the level of problem awareness and a far clearer sense of which findings are, in fact, discrepant with local objectives and mores. [emphasis added]
>
> (Huberman 1993: 13)

> In summary [. . .] the AIDS Programme can claim a wide range of applications, mostly channelled through *professional interactions between researchers and the relatively small number of practitioners* with whom they had a long term, albeit often limited, association. [emphasis added]
>
> (Mollas-Gallart *et al.* 2000: 180)

The italicized text in each of these examples highlights a similar point: the significance of sustained connections and interactions between researchers and users in enhancing research impact.

Structure of the book

The aim of Part I is to establish what user engagement is and why it is important for social science researchers and research users. In Chapter 1, we underline the significance of user engagement in terms of contemporary debates concerning research quality and relevance, knowledge production, and research use and impact. We also explain the need for greater clarity about user engagement as a concept and a process, and surface some of the key challenges and tensions that can arise in its operationalization.

Chapter 2 looks more specifically at conceptualizing user engagement in the context of educational research. A key theme is that user engagement should be seen as an opportunity for flows of knowledge from the field of study to research and from research to the field of study. We outline five broad approaches to working with users and point to their implications for project management.

In Part II, the focus shifts to a more detailed discussion of what is known about the dynamics of working with specific groups of users. Chapter 3 looks at working with practitioners and examines how researchers can manage the interface between research and practice and make the links between them as strong as possible. We discuss four strategies for engaging practitioners, and draw distinctions between approaches that emphasize knowledge sharing and those which emphasize co-construction of knowledge.

Chapter 4 considers the engagement of service users – such as children, young people, adults, families and particular groups – in and with research. Against the backdrop of increasing 'personalization' of public services, various examples of service user engagement in education and social care research and research synthesis are discussed. Tensions arising from these and other examples in the literature are considered, along with ways of managing and negotiating their impact on the engagement process.

Chapter 5 focuses on the engagement of policy-makers in research projects and with research products. We discuss what is known about the role of research in the policy process and the ways in which policy-makers can be involved in research. We focus particularly on the characteristics of research, researchers and policy-makers that can inhibit or enhance research use and the role of user engagement within this. Attention is also paid to the challenges involved in engaging policy-makers in research and how these can be overcome.

Part III provides a look forward at what can be learned for future user engagement work. Chapter 6 focuses on the implications for researchers and research processes, outlining ideas for change in four key areas: research design and project management, researcher skills and expertise, research capacity building, and research careers. Our underlying argument is that user engagement presents opportunities for new understandings of the research process and broader conceptions of what it means to be a social science researcher.

Chapter 7 outlines the key messages for research users. Four major implications are put forward, focusing on the need for better intelligence about users and engagement strategies, clearer expectations for research engagement by users, stronger capacity amongst users for research engagement, and improved infrastructure and support for user engagement.

The book ends with a short concluding note, which returns to the challenges and tensions highlighted in this introductory chapter and considers how these can best be addressed by researchers and users.

Chapter 2

Ways of thinking about user engagement

In this chapter we place the discussion of user engagement in and with educational research within broader debates about where worthwhile knowledge is produced and their implications for relationships between universities and other organizations. We use educational research as the context for our discussion while acknowledging that much of it applies equally to other areas of social science. We focus primarily on engagement *in* research and outline the different approaches to how education practitioners and other users of research become involved in research *as it is taking place*. A major theme is that user engagement should be regarded as the opportunity for flows of knowledge from the field of study to research, and from research to the field of study. We outline some of the research approaches that make user engagement a central feature and point to the implications for project management. We argue that while user engagement may bring considerable benefits for research and for the participants who are involved, it makes extra demands on everyone and calls for careful project management.

Educational research: an engaged social science

One of the starting points for the seminar series that led to this book was our strong belief that research in educational settings calls for an 'engaged social science' (Edwards 2001, 2002). By that we mean an approach to research that engages with the motivations and anticipations of the participants and the demands that they face. At the very least, it points to a way of enquiring that is sensitive to the complexities and purposes of educational practice, and, at best, it involves weaving the knowledge that arises in practice into the enquiries being pursued. We therefore saw the seminar series as an opportunity to dig below many of the assertions about user engagement and to consider its implications for different kinds of research. In doing so, we found ourselves joining a longstanding debate about the relative worth of the knowledge generated in universities when compared with knowledge generated outside academe.

Education was already caught up in that debate in relation to its usefulness for policy. As we have seen in Chapter 1, during the 1990s educational research had been regarded as the site of particularly difficult contradictions and conflicts about its purpose, and not only in the UK (Kennedy 1997; Levin 2004b; Oancea 2005; Shavelson and Towne 2002; Slavin 2002; Willinsky 2005). It seemed embroiled in a battle over whose knowledge was power in what increasingly came to be labelled the knowledge economy. Within this battle, different users placed different value on research, and the role of universities as providers of knowledge was frequently questioned. For example, in 1994, Stehr drew on Bell's (1979) observation that while academics have power within their 'intellectual institutions', they merely have influence in the larger world of policy-making, to suggest that currently experts 'at best' are part of loose associations or groups providing knowledge to those who might use it in their work.

This attention on whether knowledge generated by academics is useful has led to some quite radical questioning of how knowledge should be judged to be worthwhile and, in particular, the role of the non-scientific public in assessing its usefulness. Gibbons (1999) went so far as to suggest that there should be a trade-off between 'reliable' knowledge, and 'socially robust' knowledge with the latter being a form of public warrant for the value of research. His suggestion has considerable implications for conceptualizing the boundaries between university researchers and the worlds they study:

> [T]he more open and comprehensive the scientific community, the more socially robust will be the knowledge it produces. This is contrary to the traditional assumption that there is a strong relationship between the social and intellectual coherence (and therefore boundedness) of a scientific community and the reliability of the knowledge it produces. Reliable knowledge may have been produced by such cohesive (and therefore restricted) scientific communities. But socially robust knowledge can only be produced by much more sprawling socio/scientific constituencies with open frontiers.
>
> (C84)

Therefore, in the 1990s, at the same time as the idea of the knowledge economy was becoming common currency, the knowledge produced by researchers outside universities was set alongside the knowledge products of academe, for example, in vying for influence on policies, practices and products. One response to these shifts in the power of university expertise was to argue that the boundaries between universities and other sites of knowledge production should be eroded. Gibbons *et al.* (1994: 86) outlined what they described as 'the new production of knowledge', arguing that

> [t]he universities are no longer the remote source and well-spring of invention and creativity but, are part of the problem solving, problem identification and strategic brokering that characterize the knowledge industries.

They suggested that universities need to recognize that a change is occurring in how knowledge moves between universities and the fields in which it is brought into use. As we outlined in Chapter 1, they described the production of what they called Mode 2 knowledge to distinguish it from Mode 1 knowledge, which was the province of universities and the outcome of the conventions of knowledge production within the disciplines found in academe. Mode 2 knowledge production, in contrast, is more problem focused, trans-disciplinary and may challenge some of the more hidebound notions of what 'good science' is (3). Its production, Gibbons *et al.* argued, is based on negotiated relationships across the boundaries of universities and commercial companies aided by advances in communication technology, as teams from both settings work together to produce knowledge in the site of its application. Mode 2 knowledge therefore depends on good networks to sustain horizontal links between the sites of innovation and university researchers.

These ideas represented the zeitgeist. In 1995, Nonaki and Takeuchi wrote of the knowledge-creating company along similar lines; while Seely Brown and Duguid's widely read 2002 account of the social life of information, brought together studies of how knowledge is generated and mobilized in and amongst organizations, from a growing field of research on information in organizations. However, these discussions were not taken into educational research. Instead, during the same period, educational research found itself obliged to explain and justify its disciplinary base after the criticisms of the 1990s.

But even in studies of knowledge flows in organizations, relatively little attention was paid to the negotiations in the new spaces where knowledge from different practices came into contact. This book is, in part, an attempt to tackle this question in the context of educational research, where the practices of university research come into contact with the practices of those who work in education or use educational services. In particular, it focuses on the implications for research design that arise when trying to produce knowledge in partnerships with practitioners, service-users and policy-makers.

User engagement and educational research

We have turned the problem around from the more familiar, what use is educational research to potential users?, to instead tackle the question, what does user engagement mean for educational research? We know from our own experiences of designing research studies that, for example, incorporate conversations with users to check the validity of initial analyses and to give feedback quickly to the groups with which we work, that we need to think of user engagement in research as knowledge exchange. We also recognize that knowledge flows need to be built into research design if they are to be taken seriously. To point to the kinds of questions about knowledge exchange asked at the beginning of a study, in Table 2.1 we indicate times in the research process where different users might make particular contributions to a study.

Although the idea of knowledge exchange is central to the chapters that follow, we do not agree with the line offered by Gibbons *et al.*, (1999) that social acceptance is a major warrant for the quality of research; though we do recognize that an engaged social science should be working with what matters for the field. Rather, we are more in sympathy with Nowotny's (2000, 2003) view that specialist knowledge, and the claims for validity that go with specialist expertise, should be respected; and expert knowledge should not be diluted by the suggestion that it can be easily shared. Her solution is very much in line with the ideas put forward in this book, proposing that experts need to get closer to the fields in which their expertise is used:

Table 2.1 The potential contributions to research made by users

Users	Resources they offer to the research process	Why and when they are useful
Practitioners	Research sites, networks, ideas based on current experience	• identify practice needs for evidence • refine the research question • add detail to initial interpretations of the research problem • assist access to sites and data • keep researchers grounded and inform of changes in context and purposes of practice throughout • confirm relevance and face validity of interpretations as research continues • draw out practice implications.
Service users	Insights into their experiences of policies and practices	• identify user needs for evidence • refine the research question • add detail to initial interpretations of the research problem • keep researchers grounded and inform of changes in context • confirm relevance and face validity of interpretations as research continues • draw out implications for service.
Policy-makers/ Policy analysts	Funding, networks, policy priorities	• identify policy needs for evidence • refine the research question • contextualize the research problem throughout the process • assist access to sites and data • respond to developing conceptualizations from the research • respond to validity and relevance of findings, interpretations • draw out policy implications • broker use of research in policy.

Experts must now extend their knowledge, not simply to be an extension of what they know in their specialist field, but to consist of building links and trying to integrate what they know with what others want to, or should know and do. Bringing together the many different knowledge dimensions involved constitutes specific mixes with other kinds of knowledge, experience and expertise.

(Nowotny 2003: 155)

Our premise is that education practitioners, policy-makers, service users and researchers are expert in the practices in their own fields. The argument that follows from that premise is that educational research is likely to be enriched if some of that external expertise can be brought into play to inform it. Consequently, user engagement provides opportunities to build expert knowledge from practices in the field of study, into ongoing problem formulation and data analyses within research projects. Looked at in this way, user engagement is not an easy option but an added demand that has cost implications and calls for careful planning and sensitive negotiations.

However, educational research is a broad field that encompasses different views of what counts as acceptable knowledge and therefore different approaches to gathering it and making sense of it. For researchers whose epistemological positions take them to objectivist accounts of the relationship between research and the field of study, user engagement is likely to focus on either taking findings to policy-makers, who will in turn translate them into guidelines for practice, or to programmes of research dissemination where findings are shared with practitioners with the intention of informing their practices. There are many fine examples of these processes and, indeed, we know that policy communities would welcome even more work of this kind as their clarity can assist policy-making. However, this mode of research is also sometimes characterized as backward-looking, unable to keep pace with the more rapidly moving cycles of policy-making and not always able to prove what works.

Mulgan, writing in 2005 from his experience in the UK Prime Minister's Office, described 'policy fields in flux', which was where he placed education, in the following way:

The . . . category belongs to areas where most people recognize that things need to change; that policies which worked once are no longer working, but fewer can agree on either the diagnosis or the solutions. In these areas – a fair amount of education, some environmental policy, crime, the organization of public services – there is often a great deal of fertility and experimentation. Evidence about what works exists, but it is often patchy. It is more likely to reveal a weakness of policy and find a filter for false claims, than it is to give convincing evidence about what will work in the future.

(Mulgan 2005: 221)

Mulgan also argued for a social science version of Mode 2 knowledge production:

Today a good deal of conceptual innovation is taking place through practice, with relatively few areas in which academics develop theoretical frameworks which others then apply. More often – in cases as diverse as intelligence-led policing or drugs rehabilitation – the theorists are following behind, trying to make sense of what the practitioners are doing.

(Mulgan 2005: 223)

He seemed to be proposing that researchers who work closely with policy should become more forward-looking and focus on developing ideas alongside the practitioners who are being creatively innovative as they work on current and anticipated problems: a suggestion that certainly resonated with some of the seminar participants from policy areas.

Proponents of Mode 2 knowledge creation argue for institutional responses that blur organizational boundaries so that universities can become active partners in what Gibbons and his colleagues describe as a complex 'knowledge producing game' (Gibbons et al. 1994: 65). Knorr Cetina, writing as a sociologist of science, has started to unpack some of the complexity involved in the creation of scientific knowledge to reveal the tensions and more delicate aspects of such a 'game'. Writing of the knowledge society she described it as

a society permeated with knowledge cultures . . . The traditional definition of a knowledge society puts the emphasis on knowledge seen as scientific belief, as technological application, or perhaps as intellectual property. The definition I advocate switches the emphasis to knowledge as practised – within structures, processes and environments that make up specific epistemic settings.

(1999: 7–8)

Her premise, which she followed up in her study of knowledge construction in the European Organization for Nuclear Research (CERN) and in molecular biology laboratories, was that these epistemic cultures vary. Science is not a unity, but is comprised of diverse cultures where the different 'machineries of knowledge construction' of, for example, physicists and molecular biologists are worthy of study (1999: 3). In her study, she teased out how what these scientists know and the way they come to know it is shaped by, and shapes, their expert knowledge and practice.

Knorr Cetina gives us some useful pointers. Although researchers may be well versed in the various epistemic cultures that comprise educational research, they probably know too little about some of the epistemic cultures that comprise education as it is practised, and the same is likely to be true of how other practitioners understand research. The practices of education, like the practices of laboratory scientists, are likely to be diverse and need to be understood and brought into knowledge construction processes for mutual learning across research–practice boundaries. As Gibbons (1999: C83) explains, 'experts must now . . . try to integrate what they "know" now with what others want to "do" in the future.' That is, researchers who work on practices need to have strong links with the fields of study if they are to engage with its practices, anticipations and emergent challenges and to offer insights that might inform the way the field is able to look to the future.

Close connections with practices as they developed to tackle new problems also lay behind the TLRP requirement that user engagement should be a feature of every project in the programme. However, user engagement within forward-looking constructivist accounts of educational research is, like constructivism itself, not easily categorized. In what follows, we tease out some different approaches to user engagement and knowledge exchange that are to be found within more interpretative modes of educational research.

Five broad approaches to user engagement

'User engagement' is not just a clumsy term: it is also demeaning, almost denying the expertise that participants who are not professional researchers can bring to a piece of engaged social science. Our premise, that researchers need to see collaborations with people who are not primarily researchers as a knowledge exchange, was an attempt to overcome some of the hidden biases in the term. However, when we looked across the different approaches to research in collaboration with people who would also use the research, we found differences in the nature of the relationships. These differences centred on who controlled the research and where the boundaries around a research study were drawn. We shall examine five approaches to working with users in research:

- creating feedback loops
- university-led participatory research
- combining small-scale studies
- co-research for conceptual development
- user-led research.

The first and last approaches were not represented in the TLRP; the remaining three were evident. The first two approaches can be characterized as processes of knowledge exchange across the boundaries of different practices. The remaining three approaches go further than just exchanging knowledge to include some kind of co-construction that involves practitioners, policy-makers or service users who are not professional researchers, in processes of knowledge construction in research partnerships.

Creating feedback loops

This approach to user engagement does not involve participants working as researchers, but it does attempt to keep them engaged with the research as it develops. It does this by maintaining flows of knowledge between the field and the project through presenting emerging findings to participants at regular intervals and asking for feedback. The boundary between a research project and participants in the research is quite firmly drawn and researchers take research-based knowledge to the boundary where it is presented to participants.

Presenting emerging findings to participants has three advantages for the project: it is a check on the immediate face validity of developing interpretations, it is ethically appropriate to pass findings that might be relevant back to the field as quickly as possible and the discussions that ensue at feedback meetings provide additional data.

However, feedback loops need to be planned for and to be built into the design of the study. It is therefore useful to ask the following questions when a study is being planned as they have implications for research design, for ethical approval and for how entry into the field is negotiated:

- How can each group of participants inform the development of the research?
- Which of the participants would like to know what?
- How do we time the feedback?
- How do we deal with confidentiality and anonymity?
- Do we expect participants to act on the knowledge we are sharing during the research process?
- When will we have findings that are robust enough to share more widely beyond the participant groups?
- Will we involve participants in the wider knowledge sharing?

Providing.feedback during a research study is not a new process: reflexivity between researcher and researched has long been regarded as both ethically appropriate and likely to enhance the quality of the research from people's experiences. However, working through a list of questions like these can help early career researchers to judge the degree of professional distance that they intend to assume and to assess the time implications of presenting interim findings and setting up meetings. Creating feedback loops is particularly relevant when researching in an area like education, where the environment changes and priorities frequently shift, making it important for researchers to keep up to date.

University-led participatory research

In this model of research, users such as teachers may be involved in the research process as field testers who, for example, try out material developed by researchers. They may help to refine artefacts for use in classrooms, and talk with other teachers about what they have done. There is a strong tradition of this mode of working within science education research (e.g. Harlen 1977; Millar 2002). This approach has a great deal in common with the curriculum development intentions of design experiments (Brown 1992; Collins 1992; Ruthven *et al.* 2009), which we discuss in Chapter 3.

Another way of participating in university-led studies is through joining expert panels who give feedback on ideas being developed by researchers. User involvement for field-based practitioners can therefore include comments on research instruments, some data collection while artefacts are trialled or ideas tried out and help with dissemination. The TLRP also encouraged the use of expert panels, which included representatives of policy communities, to help projects keep up to date with the changing policy priorities in the fields they were studying.

In this approach to participation, a boundary is drawn firmly around a core research team, with the field testers or expert panels being invited into the core team to inform the project at predetermined times. The purpose of the study and its timescale are entirely set by the university teams and the boundaries are also managed by them. Users' expertise is regarded as making a valuable contribution to research projects and their feedback is woven into changes in the knowledge products being developed, but the users are brought into the service of the study and do not contribute to shaping its design. They frequently report enjoying the experience; that they are learning; and, in the case of practitioners, that they feel they are making important contributions to their area of professional interest.

The contribution of these potential users of the research products makes demands on project management. Nonetheless, it is highly valued because of its impact on the relevance of, for example, the curriculum guidelines that are produced. User warrants ensure that research products are likely to be acceptable to user communities, which in turn help with scaling up the research findings to more broadly inform services and practices.

Combining small-scale studies

Several TLRP projects used action research as part of their research design (e.g. Ainscow *et al.* 2006; Sutherland *et al.* 2007). Here the practitioners' studies taking place in schools and local authorities were included within the boundary of the broader research project. However, this approach was not without its tensions. Although research projects taking this approach usually give some freedom of movement to the teachers or other users involved to develop their own investigations in their own schools or services, the smaller studies are finally embedded in larger-scale projects, which are led by university-based staff towards meeting the research objectives that are the condition of their funding. Ideas are tested and developed in schools or classrooms by teachers in cycles of development that also involve the university-based research teams. As a result, larger-scale studies that include action research methods often operate with complex iterative research designs which have a great deal in common with tightly focused design experiments (Cobb *et al.* 2003). This is discussed in Chapter 3.

The tensions that can arise in projects made up of a number of smaller studies can raise important questions for the development of user engagement in large-scale projects. One is the question of who controls the research. For example, it is essential that classroom practitioners or service users see the time that they spend on the research as being worthwhile; equally, it is essential to the wider projects and the objectives that researchers are obliged to meet, that practitioners and service users really do engage with the developments that are being tested.

New relationships between university researchers and practitioner and service user researchers therefore need to be negotiated. For instance, because the practitioner or service user research is so central to the designs of the larger projects, hierarchies of responsibility and expertise between professional researchers and practitioner or service user researchers can become blurred. This blurring can create tensions for the university-based researchers between being responsive to changes affecting practitioner or service user communities, while remaining faithful to the research designs for which they were responsible. In one TLRP project, practitioner-researchers found the work to be so relevant that it was difficult to see how the research team could place limits on the spread of the study to other teachers and other schools, and deal with the consequent demands on their time within the constraints of project funding.

Co-research for conceptual development

There was only one example of this model of research in TLRP (Edwards *et al.* 2009a). It aimed at developing and refining concepts that helped to explain and take forward understandings of changing practices. It was different from action research studies because the research team was not working with practitioners to test developments in practices, but to generate fresh ways of explaining what was going on in existing and emerging practices within relatively long-term partnerships. For the main part of the study, the team worked in three case study sites and one senior practitioner from each site was seconded part-time to the research.

The team used methods from Developmental Work Research (DWR) (Engeström 2007) to reveal the knowledge that was embedded in new (inter-professional) practices as they developed. The process is described in Chapter 3. In brief, the team worked with groups of practitioners over time. It shared the analytic tools it used in the study with the practitioners to help them to explain their own developing work practices and take forward their own understandings of that practice. The boundary around the project included both researchers and participants. However, the researchers, with the seconded practitioners, were responsible for setting the agenda, organizing meetings and undertaking analyses.

DWR is a powerful and challenging mode of working and therefore requires strong participant commitment to the processes. The team found that if participants were not interested in rethinking their practices and exploring developments in relation to their institutional systems, they would dislike the process. The powerful analytic tools offered in the DWR process and the contradictions they unearthed would be resisted. Even where there was an interest amongst practitioners, participants needed to become gradually aware of how DWR could disrupt assumptions and lead to some quite profound changes in understandings of practice. Once the DWR process started it allowed rapid feedback of ongoing analyses to participants through presenting evidence from the field as stimulus material for further analytic discussions. At the same time, the sessions allowed reflexivity, as participants could question interpretations and offer alternatives. The research team facilitator was simply one voice in these multi-voiced settings and he or she focused on capturing the contradictions that arose when the stimulus data were discussed, rather than asserting the research team's interpretation as the most valid.

Other studies, for example, the DETAIL project with English teachers (Ellis 2010) and the National Evaluation of the Children's Fund (Edwards *et al.* 2006a), have used lighter versions of DWR for evidence-based sessions that are designed specifically to stimulate user engagement in working with the data, in order to reveal for participants both their own 'personal sense-making' and any contradictions in the systems in which they work.

User-led research

User-led research is not often funded by the UK research funding councils because their funding goes only to universities or equivalent organizations. However, there are examples of user-led research to be found. These include work on disabilities led by professional, university-based researchers who are also living with disability – Shakespeare's (1993, 2006) work is a prime example here. But it also encompasses research relationships like the direct involvement of the Suresearch network (www.suresearch.org.uk) of mental health service users as researchers in projects undertaken by the Institute of Applied Social Studies, University of Birmingham.

The Suresearch example is particularly interesting as the members of Suresearch have gradually developed research skills over time through sustained involvement in studies with members of the institute. They work within project boundaries as full members of research teams, both undertaking fieldwork and contributing to analyses alongside university research staff. They are also powerful communicators of research outcomes, able to clearly point to the potential impact of findings. Importantly, user-led research of this kind is quite different from research that aims at giving voice to the less privileged, where these voices are unavoidably filtered through the analytic lenses of the authors of the texts.

Of course, research users may also be funders. In those cases, users are heavily involved in early negotiations on the scope and shape of the research with research teams. Government departments and a few of the charitable foundations (e.g. the Nuffield Foundation) are probably major examples of this kind of relationship. But although they continue to offer expert advice during the study, they rarely engage in research alongside professional researchers. Funders' requirements in the application process that cover user engagement are explored in more detail in Chapter 7.

Summary

These five approaches paint a broad picture of options for user engagement in research and there are, of course, nuanced differences to be found within each category. There are also important differences amongst them. The first two approaches (creating feedback loops and university-led participatory research), although within an interpretative or constructivist framing of research, have strong traces of more objectivist stances. The research is often done on the participants and their expertise is brought into play to serve a predetermined research agenda around which there is a firm boundary. The remaining three approaches are more likely to meet Gibbons' criterion of experts, in this case researchers, trying 'to integrate what they "know" now with what others want to "do" in the future' (1999: C83).

The discussion of the third approach (combining small-scale studies), has pointed to the challenges of moving away from tight university control over processes and giving a high degree of freedom of action to practitioner/service user participants. However, these difficulties seem to arise mainly from the constraints of the funders' requirement that final reports show how studies have reached predetermined objectives. We would suggest that working more flexibly with the users of research knowledge should be supported by a funding system that recognizes that the changing world of practice will give rise to changing objects of enquiry.

The fourth approach (co-research for conceptual development) places the research team overtly in charge of the agenda, but an important part of the methodology is to give the analytic tools to the participants so that they can analyse their own work situations. It is expected that these resources remain useful once projects have ended. The final approach (user-led research), and in particular the Suresearch example, illustrates the impact of long-term investment in training potential users in research processes and a melding of both researcher and user expertise within the same person. As well as these differences, a comparison of these approaches also reveals some strong themes in relation to the management of research studies and it is to these that we now turn.

Challenges for project management

As we have already indicated, we see user engagement in research as the bringing together of different practices, each with its specialist expertise and value-laden goals, in a common endeavour. The approaches we have just outlined deal with the movement of knowledge between intersecting practices differently. In research which simply creates feedback loops and to an extent in university-led research, knowledge is negotiated across boundaries between research and professional practices; in the other three approaches, knowledge is negotiated within research projects that operate as sites of intersecting practices where new understandings are co-constructed.

Whatever the approach, user engagement and the management of knowledge in research projects need to be orchestrated. Project management therefore becomes an important task that includes:

- acknowledging and weaving together the different purposes of research for different participants;
- planning for different timescales for each group of participants;
- developing new forms of relational expertise that strengthen mutual engagement in and with research.

Different purposes

Seeing user engagement as the orchestration of different forms of expertise to accomplish a research task, means that it is rather like interdisciplinary research. Interdisciplinary research has become more important as the complexities of social problems are increasingly recognized and it may bring together, for example, social scientists, software engineers and natural scientists. Each will interpret the research problem differently as they bring their particular expertise into play and will engage with it for slightly different reasons. Project management is therefore crucial in this kind of research project, not only to coordinate the planning of specialist teams, but also to build common understandings of the long-term purpose of the work. Sharing an understanding of the goals of the study can operate as a kind of glue that holds together disparate groups when compromises inevitably need to be made. This is as true of studies that incorporate potential users as of other forms of interdisciplinary research.

We would suggest, therefore, that time needs to be spent building common knowledge (Carlile 2004; Edwards in press). Carlile observes how common knowledge as the basis of potential collaboration represents the motives in practices when he describes it as having the 'capacity . . . to represent the differences and dependencies now of consequence and the ability of the actors involved to use it' (2004: 557). Creating common knowledge is therefore not simply a matter of building enough shared knowledge to enable people to work together, it also involves taking the time to discover what a project means for each group of participants, why they are involved in it and what matters most for them as they take time to do the work. Obvious differences in purposes are the university researchers' need to maintain an academic reputation by achieving research objectives and by publishing for other academics, while practitioner motives are shaped by the priorities of their workplaces – for example, whether they are schools or local authorities. Project management therefore involves helping people make these purposes explicit, ensuring respect for different motives and weaving them together so that a project is completed on time while addressing the purposes of participants.

Different timescales

Academics usually approach research projects with a strong sense of timescale. Research bids require detailed timetables and agreed milestones. Yet one of the advantages of user engagement for educational research is that the insights that field-based experts bring can reveal unexpected research trails and new ideas to pursue. Accessing these insights is part of the process of working alongside practitioners to engage with anticipations as they arise and it can disrupt the best-laid research plans. Project management therefore involves carefully considered trade-offs between emerging lines of enquiry enriched by user engagement, and the need to meet research objectives that may have become outmoded as a result of these insights.

Different timescales also occur as a result of different rhythms in the organizations in which participants are based. School holidays can be planned into research projects but unannounced inspections or staffing crises cannot. Action research projects also bring special demands as they are often difficult to bring to an end, since participants work through cycle after cycle, engrossed by the developments that arise. A sharing of common purposes makes negotiations around timescales a little easier, but it is a problem that besets all kinds of interdisciplinary research.

New forms of relational expertise in project management

We have been emphasizing that user engagement involves bringing together different types of expertise and specialist knowledge and that project management is a matter of negotiating relevant knowledge into projects and back out into the field. The expertise and knowledge that users can bring to the research processes needs to be elicited, collected and incorporated into the development of projects. This is a coordination job that calls for specific skills.

Project management as we have described it involves brokering knowledge in and out of different practices. This brokering, we suggest, demands a form of relational expertise: the ability to recognize and work with the specialist knowledge and professional motives of others. At the core of this form of expertise is the ability to 'know how to know who' (can help with what). We are not alone in this suggestion. Lundvall (1996; 2000) has identified 'know who' as a much needed new capability alongside the 'know what', 'know why' and 'know how' of professional competence because 'it involves the social capacity to establish relationships to specialized groups in order to draw on their expertise' (1996: 8). These relationships are part of the social practices of systems and are often informal, hence, suggests Lundvall, big firms do basic research because it gives them access to informal relationships with scientists. We think that the same is true of relationships in education. Therefore, if know who is important for making the most of user engagement, it needs to be labelled and acknowledged in strategies for building research capacity.

Of course, for 'know who' to enhance horizontal knowledge flows between the fields of practice and research, conditions need to be created to allow it to develop. In the first two of the approaches discussed in this chapter, researchers set up fora at the boundaries of projects and exchanged information there. In the other three approaches, practitioners were more directly involved in team meetings, enabling common knowledge to be built, a stronger sense of what each group could contribute to be achieved and specialist networks to be made available. Even more challenging than enabling horizontal knowledge flows between operational-level users and university-based researchers, is the task of moving knowledge upstream from educational research to inform national policies through the engagement of policy-makers. We tackle this topic in more detail in Chapter 5. Here we simply point to the relevance of what has been learned from horizontal links between practitioner users of research and research projects.

The practice of policy-making and implementation is very different from the practice of research. There may be overlapping purposes, children's well-being or scientific literacy for example, but decisions are also made for other purposes in both sets of practices. The timescales are also clearly different, with policy-makers, for example, often having to operate with less than perfect data to meet timeframes set by government. Relational expertise is a useful attribute for researchers to develop if it means they become better positioned to recognize and work with the motives of policy-makers as they negotiate their findings into policy contexts. In the seminar series, we discussed the creation of sustained fora where researchers and policy specialists could meet, where both know who and common knowledge could be built. These ideas were welcomed by members of policy communities and there was clearly evidence of this being more likely to happen in smaller national or local systems than in larger systems.

Summary

In this chapter, we have set out a conceptual framework for discussing user engagement in research and its implications for research strategies. We will discuss the details of research design in the chapters that follow. Here, we have simply outlined five broad approaches to working with those who are also likely to use the knowledge generated in the research:

- creating feedback loops
- university-led participatory research
- combining small-scale studies
- co-research for conceptual development
- user-led research.

When we looked across the different approaches to research in collaboration with people who would also use the research, we found differences in the nature of the relationships. These differences centred on who controlled the research and on where the boundaries around a research study were drawn. However, all the approaches gave rise to similar challenges:

- acknowledging and weaving together the different purposes of research for different participants;

- planning for different timescales for each group of participants;
- developing new forms of relational expertise that strengthen mutual engagement in and with research.

These challenges led us to emphasize the importance of project management in user engagement.

PART II

WHAT DOES THE RESEARCH SAY?

Chapter 3

Engaging practitioners

This chapter is about why researchers work with field-based practitioners and how they can do it. Its main focus is therefore what researchers need to be able to do if they are to maintain close links with practitioners and the fields they are studying throughout the research process. In Chapter 2, we discussed how research spirals in and out of its fields of study and argued that it needs to do this in ways that benefit not only the research study, but also the participants and the fields in which they are working. Therefore, although this chapter is not a guide to how practitioners engage in and with research, by examining how researchers can manage the interface between research and practice, it is concerned with making the links between research and practice as strong as possible. Our focus is the design and conduct of studies with permeable boundaries that allow an easy flow of knowledge from practices into projects and from research into practices.

Working with practitioners in research projects

The TLRP was exceptional in requesting that every project in the programme set out its plans for engaging research users. We have outlined the different ways this was tackled in the models we discussed in Chapter 2. In this chapter, we examine in more detail why and how researchers and field-based practitioners collaborate in research.

Who are the practitioners?

The ideas in this book have been developed in the context of discussions about user engagement in and with educational research, particularly on learning and teaching. The processes of learning and teaching are, of course, at the heart of the practices to be found, for example, in schools, colleges, universities and professional development services. Therefore, the practitioners who are the focus of this chapter are people who are involved in guiding the learning of others shaping the environments in which learning occurs through their strategic or management roles, or supporting the well-being of learners. They work in organizations that have educational aims, but they may not always work in settings that would be recognized as formal education, and their roles in the research process run the gamut of possibilities outlined in the five models of research we discussed in Chapter 2. Working closely with busy practitioners in research takes time and energy, yet we see these research relationships as mutually beneficial. At the very least, this is because researchers and practitioners who work on teaching and learning share the common aim of enhancing learning through understanding and developing the practices that support it.

Our focus on relationships between the development of practices and research means that when we discuss practitioners in this chapter we are not talking about the lone heroic practitioner-researcher who works against the grain of local practices to reveal and solve problems. Instead, we are thinking more collectively. The central research relationship, we suggest, needs to be between research projects and educational organizations such as schools, subject departments or a local authority service, rather than with individual practitioners. Researchers might work with individuals, but our experience tells us that unless the project is negotiated at the level of the organization in which the practitioners are employed, the impact of the research on practice is likely to be limited and the freedom for practitioners to work with researchers in a sustained way is often curtailed.

Why is working together important for practitioners and educational researchers?

If research on teaching and learning is to be relevant to the field, the knowledge and values that are embedded in the practices of education professionals need to be the starting point and the continuing reference point for studies. This is not an argument for limiting research to the description of what is already there. Rather, it is an invitation for researchers and practitioners to explore ways of working together so that both can expand their understandings of what is involved in teaching and how it can be developed to enhance learning. This invitation offers a considerable challenge to education as a social science, but it is not a new one. We shall rehearse the challenge here as it will be the touchstone for evaluating the approaches we later suggest.

First, we need be clear about how we are using the terms 'practice' and 'practitioner'. In this chapter, organizations, such as schools, are seen as made up of practices that are inhabited by teachers, teaching assistants and so on. These practices are knowledge-laden and shaped by values and organizational history. Practitioners become expert in working within specific practices to take forward their aims, and their professional identities often become bound up in them.

All of these features make practices both fascinating to study and very difficult to change, as new knowledge is often so heavily filtered and adapted to fit historical practices that it becomes unrecognizable. The key to changing practices, encouraging the generation of knowledge and the productive use of relevant new knowledge is therefore to legitimize the questioning of practices and, indeed, build such questioning into the practices themselves. It is for this reason that we are taking a collective rather than individual approach to understanding research relationships with practitioners; it is very difficult to scrutinize practices in organizations that don't encourage it.

The questioning of organizational practices calls for what Evetts (2009) has described as 'occupational professionalism', which she contrasts with 'organizational professionalism' where practitioners' actions are shaped by routines that demand little in the way of professional judgement. Occupational professionalism, alternatively, calls for judgement and an awareness of values and purposes in practices. Webb (2002) noted that expert systems such as evidence-based practice attempt to manufacture trust by legitimizing a mandate for professional practice, thus reducing the likelihood that practitioners can reflect on and evaluate their own practice.

Opening up practices to scrutiny

Evetts' distinction and emphasis on judgement very usefully connects with the challenge to social science set out by Flyvbjerg (2001), who argued that social science 'is locked in a fight it cannot hope to win because it has accepted terms that are self-defeating' (3). The impossibility of the task lies, he suggested, in social science's attempts to be as effective as the natural sciences in producing theories that are powerfully explanatory and can be applied with predictable results. His argument was that social sciences are, however, stronger in an area where the natural sciences are weak: that is, in 'the reflexive analysis and discussion of values and interests, which is the prerequisite for an enlightened political, economic, and cultural development of any society' (3).

Labelling this attribute 'phronesis', he argued that this is more than either analytic scientific knowledge or technical or know-how knowledge and that it is a common aspect of social practices. The connection with occupational professionalism is clear in Aristotle's description of phronesis, which is heavily value-laden. Flyvbjerg gives Aristotle's definition as a 'true state, reasoned, and capable of action with regard to things that are good or bad for man' (2001: 2). Interpreting the role of educational research as engagement with phronesis emphasizes its educational purpose: it is there to inform professional judgements that occur within knowledge-laden and values-driven practices. How knowledge enters those practices is, of course, a key question and one that we shall attempt to answer from the perspective of research relationships.

Building prototypes of practices

We see the practice of educational research as distinct from, and complementary to, practices such as teaching and managing education. The practice of educational research, like any other expert practice, is imbued with motives and laden with knowledge. However, whenever practices are brought together so that practitioners can work in parallel on a shared concern, the challenge is that each practitioner needs to understand enough about what matters for the others to enable them to align their practices and work together. Elsewhere, one of us has discussed this in terms of relational expertise (Edwards in press). This kind of expertise involves the ability to look across the boundaries of specialist practice to recognize that both practices share the same values but might look at problems in different ways, and that both have specialist knowledge that can usefully be brought to bear on the problems they are working on together, in what we are calling 'close-to-practice' research.

Nissen (2009) has been developing similar ideas with his suggestion that researchers and practitioners can collaborate in what he calls 'practice research' to create 'prototypes' in the course of dialogues between the practice of research and, in his example, the practice of social work. He argues that the practice of research allows the everyday practices of different kinds of social work to be turned into objects of study and examined by researchers and social workers. This collaborative examination allows them to jointly build 'models' or accounts of what is going on.

The model or account of the practices can then be scrutinized by quite openly employing the theoretical tools brought by the researchers to explore what Nissen calls 'general issues, relations, problems, possibilities, etc., for which the particular social work practice is claimed to be prototypical' (2009: 76). These prototypes are therefore not simply models of what is there but carry in them the possibility of looking forward, generating new questions and remaining open to scrutiny and change. In his case, Nissen has developed the prototype of 'wild social work' as something easily recognizable but also open to change. His is a complex and subtle argument, which is not easily summarized, but his core point is that 'the relationship between researchers and practitioners is an intersubjective relationship in which both are participants' (68) and that the resources that researchers bring allow what is so often hidden in practices to surface. The outcome is not simply the development of practices but new understandings of practices that are informed by those who inhabit them.

Working at the interface of the practices of research and education

In summary, our argument in this chapter is that research relationships with educational practitioners, (i) can be seen as phronesis through opening up practices for scrutiny and involving practitioners in the activity; and following Nissen, (ii) can give rise to potentially powerful prototypes that are refined as they are used to analyse practices. We are therefore not about to discuss how individual teachers can engage in action research or independent study. Rather, we are focusing on research relationships across the specialist practices of research and education to the mutual benefit of both.

Our interest in how researchers can understand and work at the interface between research and practice fits quite closely with the 'organizational excellence' model of research use offered by Morris *et al.* in their 2007 review of how research and development can be designed to influence practice (Box 3.1).

Box 3.1 Three models of research use

Research-based practitioner model

- It is the role and responsibility of the individual practitioner to keep abreast of research and to ensure that it is used to inform day-to-day practice.
- The use of research is a linear process of accessing, appraising and applying research.
- Practitioners have high levels of professional autonomy to change practice based on research.
- Professional education and training are important in enabling research use.

Embedded-research model

- Research use is achieved by embedding research in the systems and processes of social care, such as standards, policies, procedures and tools.
- Responsibility for ensuring research use lies with policy makers and service delivery managers.
- The use of research is both a linear and an instrumental process: research is translated directly into practice change.
- Funding, performance management and regulatory regimes are used to encourage the use of research-based guidance and tools.

Organizational excellence model

- The key to successful research use rests with social care delivery organizations – their leadership, management and organization.
- Research use is supported by developing an organizational culture that is 'research-minded'.
- There is local adaptation of research findings and ongoing learning within organizations.
- Partnership with local universities and intermediary organizations are used to facilitate both the creation and use of research knowledge.

Source: Walter *et al.* 2004: 25–6 in Morris *et al.* 2007: 10

Nutley *et al.* (2007: 5–6) used the three models shown in Box 3.1 to examine 'contrasting approaches to evidence creating and practitioner use' (of research) across health care, social care, education and criminal justice. The comparison revealed that in education there is 'considerable focus on [the] "research-based practitioner" model but also significant investments in interactive and collaborative approaches to research use' (6). It appears from their analysis that more attention needs to be paid to organizational excellence approaches to engagement with research and to phronesis.

However, the phronesis argument is not only beneficial for educational practice and practitioners; it is also, as Flyvbjerg suggests, a way out of a self-defeating impasse for those social sciences that work with practices. We made a similar point in Chapter 2 when we argued that pedagogic research in education could be seen as an engaged social science and discussed how the co-construction of knowledge in research in the TLRP mirrored the kinds of partnerships between university and workplace-based researchers that characterize Mode 2 knowledge production (Gibbons *et al.* 1994).

Planning close-to-practice research

We suggest that much more needs to be known about the relationships necessary for pedagogic research in education to function as a close-to-practice social science. In this chapter we attempt to unpack the different relationships and their implications for research studies. Let us start with some quite general points. Morris *et al.* (2007) identified three areas of responsibility for researchers who wanted to work with practitioners and influence practice: planning, managing and influencing. The points they made are summarized in Box 3.2.

Box 3.2   Planning, managing and influencing research

Principles for planning

- Consult key stakeholders about research priorities.
- Explore opportunities for synthesizing existing research findings.
- Consider partnering possibilities with key stakeholders.
- Identify and include end-users in Project Advisory Groups.
- Consider research impact at project design stage.

Principles for managing

- Keep potential end-users informed of progress during projects.
- Involve end-users in discussing findings and implications for practice.
- Explore opportunities for 'co-production' of research.

Principles for influencing

- Develop easy-to-use, searchable databases of research projects.
- Explore dissemination with partner/intermediary organizations.
- Encourage different outputs tailored for different end-users.
- Emphasize tailored dissemination and communication strategies.
- Create opportunities for discussion of findings/implications.
- Support research outputs that take account of users' needs/ contexts.

Source: Morris *et al.* 2007: 2

The principles outlined are together a useful list of pointers for researchers who are about to embark on a study. They recognize that research relationships with practitioners may come in many forms and are not simply linear processes where research findings are produced and then applied. Nonetheless, the points retain an emphasis on the end use of the products of research and underplay how engaging in research with practitioners can be mutually informing throughout the research process. Our suggestion that shifting the emphasis to how both research and practice can be mutually informed during a research study – is based on four assumptions:

- The relationship between research studies and fields of practice is not a simple linear one: it is complex and needs careful management over time.
- Working closely with the field of practice can strengthen educational research as it allows researchers to keep in touch with current intentions in practices.
- Engagement in research alongside university-based researchers can help educational practitioners to create a capacity for purposeful questioning of practices and sustaining innovation.
- The word 'relationship' is important: knowledge is mobilized and shared in conversations where each participant recognizes what is important for the others in the conversation.

There are two broad approaches for researchers to select from when working with these assumptions. One is to see the relationship in terms of efficient knowledge flows between the practice of research and educational practices. The other is to see the relationships amongst practices as aiming at the co-construction of knowledge, in line, for example, with Nissen's (2009) notion of prototypes. Each broad approach calls for a different aide-memoire for researchers to help them plan their studies.

Knowledge flows

One way of working with the assumptions we have just listed is to think of research and educational work as two different practices where care needs to be taken to manage knowledge across practice boundaries. This response leads to an aide-memoire that is based on the principles of knowledge exchange. These principles give rise to design issues that require researchers to identify:

- why a cross-boundary knowledge flow between practices is necessary for their study;
- when knowledge should move across research-practice boundaries.

The answers to these considerations then begin to shape the design of the study and in particular the need to plan for meetings at certain points. However, as all educators know, a good plan is not enough: the learning process needs to be guided. Therefore, the second step in the design of a research study based on knowledge exchange is to recognize that the guidance that comes from project management is crucial. The next part of the knowledge exchange aide-memoire therefore includes the following considerations:

- who manages the interface where research and educational practices meet;
- who meets at it;
- whether different groups need to meet at different times in the research process;
- how research-based and practice-based knowledge should be represented at meetings;
- how these meetings can be used to further inform research and practice.

Co-construction

An alternative to the knowledge management approach to practitioner engagement in research studies is to see it more as an ongoing process of co-construction of knowledge within field-based educational practices. Here researchers and practitioners may have different roles based on their specific expertise, but they are in constant contact, working together towards a shared understanding of what is going on in practices. The aide-memoire for co-construction research should include the following questions.

- Has everyone agreed on the overarching purpose of the study?
- Does everyone understand the demands of this kind of research partnership?
- Has the school, college or other research site signed up to ensuring that these demands can be accommodated?
- Are different roles and responsibilities clear and agreed upon?
- Have the boundaries of the work been made clear; that is, that this is a research project with time limits and objectives to meet?
- Is the timetable for research activity and interim outputs clear?
- Have all aspects of writing up the findings been discussed?

Strategies for engaging with practitioners in research

These two aides-memoires give some broad suggestions as to how to plan for practitioner engagement in different kinds of research projects. We now turn to four specific strategies for engaging practitioners in research:

- making knowledge exchange a central feature of research design;
- building a research study from action research projects;
- design experiments and didactical design;
- Developmental Work Research (DWR).

Making knowledge exchange a central feature of research design

This strategy lends itself to some kinds of evaluation and to curriculum development studies where the intention is to inform practice as well as make judgements about it. A number of research designs have knowledge exchange as a core element. Theories of Change (Connell and Kubisch 1998) is one prominent example of an evaluation design that has knowledge-sharing at its core. Designed as an approach to evaluating community initiatives, by requiring researchers to identify and follow the theories of change held by different stakeholders in an initiative, it has also been described as 'a powerful tool for promoting collaboration and engagement at the community level focused on products and outcomes' (Connell and Kubisch 1998: ʃ12). Conversations between researchers and stakeholders about the intentions of participants in initiatives and what strategies they are using to achieve their goals are central to the research approach. Connell and Kubisch therefore suggest that one of its strengths lies in how it can be used to educate and mobilize participants in the initiative as it 'helps to make explicit the capacity-building agenda of the initiative and the role evaluation can play in that agenda' (1998: ʃ12).

Sullivan *et al.* (2002) have more explicitly made that argument in their discussion of using Theories of Change in an evaluation of Health Action Zones (HAZ). There they describe the strategy as 'co-research' in a way that matches exactly our argument that research relationships between university researchers and field-based practitioners allow the bringing together of two kinds of expertise for the benefit of all. Although they are discussing relationships with service users as well as with practitioners, they do illustrate the advantages we have been outlining in this chapter on working with practitioners:

> Co-research is complementary to 'theories of change' as it too prioritizes a direct relationship between evaluator and HAZ and it seeks to develop the research framework through a process of exchange between the two. The evaluators bring to the table knowledge and expertise drawn from previous research, while the HAZs bring knowledge and expertise drawn from their experience of implementing HAZ in their locality.
>
> (Sullivan *et al.* 2002: 220)

In other less explicitly participatory strategies for research on and in practices, reflexivity between research site and practice still has clear advantages for all involved. For example, the benefits of simply building feedback and discussion fora, where researchers and participants meet, into a research design can be summarized as follows:

- It is ethically sound, as it ensures that interim analyses are given back to research participants and co-researchers and can be used by them while they are still relevant.
- It assists validity, as participants and co-researchers can check the account being constructed and point out misconceptions.
- The discussions involved in the responses to the interim analyses can be captured as additional data, which allow an even stronger understanding of what matters in the practices being researched.

With these three benefits in mind, one of us has used a light version of DWR (Engeström 2007), which is discussed later in this chapter, to structure feedback sessions to the schools that had been the case studies in an exploration of new welfare roles in secondary schools (Edwards *et al.* 2010). The research team undertook an interim analysis of the data from each school. Analyses were then taken back to the specific school as material to be shared and reflected on together by the participants in the study, in two-hour structured discussions. After getting the permission of people whose words were to be used, the findings were represented to the group through quotes from interviews, which illustrated more general themes or contradictions, and by graphical models of how the welfare system of the school appeared to be developing.

The reflections in the sessions were shaped by questions about the purposes of the schools' practices, the changing division of labour and the implicit and explicit rules in place: all of which owe a great deal to activity theory (Engeström 1999, see p. 58 in this chapter). The discussions were also recorded and subsequently helped to refine the research team's final analyses, which were again fed back. In this example, the agenda was clearly managed by the research team, who built reflexivity into a funded study that had fixed objectives and a rigid timescale. Influencing practices so that phronesis can become embedded in them is therefore not one of the aims of this approach. Yet the intention in the welfare roles study was to mutually inform both research and school practices through an exchange of knowledge that included not only the findings, but also a way of interrogating practices by asking questions about the division of labour, rules and so on.

We are not suggesting that there is a blueprint for designing for reflexivity and knowledge exchange. We are suggesting that following the knowledge exchange aide-memoire outlined in the previous section will help with planning for it. Our emphasis on planning also means that we don't think knowledge exchange can simply be a bolt-on or extra element in a study. Rather, it needs to be integrated into the study so that projects are designed to take advantage of what is learned in the fora.

Building a research study from action research projects

This has become a popular strategy for research on teaching and learning because it is seen as bringing together the expertise that is found in both research and educational practice and gives a very clear role in the research process for education-based participants. The research projects usually consist of several action research studies around a common theme such as assessment in English or teaching 'proof' in mathematics. The idea is that practitioners work on their small-scale individual projects while being part of the wider thematic project. Each individual study is a single case study of, for example, a piece of curriculum development, and the wider project allows for both mutual support and cross-case comparisons through which broader principles can be recognized and shared more widely.

The TLRP Using Computers to Enhance Learning study (Sutherland *et al.* 2007) is a good example of a study designed explicitly as a partnership between university researchers, teacher educators and teachers. It aimed not only at finding out about how information and communications technology (ICT) could be used to support pedagogy, but also at integrating ICT into everyday classroom practices. It involved four primary schools, five secondary schools and a further education college, fifty-nine teachers, seven researchers, six teacher educators and three research students who were all placed in Subject Design Teams (SDTs) in English, mathematics, science, modern foreign languages, music, history and geography with university-based staff. The SDTs worked together in the schools to develop and evaluate examples of practice that showed how ICT could be used as a tool for learning.

The study was informed conceptually by sociocultural accounts of learning as mediated by tools that were brought to the study by the research team. Each SDT, though, was charged with designing, developing and evaluating a way of working with ICT to promote pupil learning, and in that process drew on the 'plan → act → review' principles of an action research study. However, the study was far more than a series of action research projects, as the framework provided by the overarching university-led project meant that individual studies could be compared across the project and general principles could be drawn about the pedagogic use of ICT. Though the team did not draw on Nissen's (2009) notion of prototypes as generative models of practice, they did create them and in the dialogic way that he outlines.

There was also an impact on practitioners, which returns us to the discussion of phronesis. Here are two practitioners' accounts of their experiences in the study taken from the project's research briefing paper (TLRP 2006):

> It was encouraging . . . we're all trying to work it through together. If you had a lot of experts going 'this, this, this and this and English and ICT works well in this particular way' I think this would be daunting to the rest of us.
>
> (3, partner-teacher)

> Working closely with my university partner and the whole team was without doubt the biggest influence on my learning. I was introduced to new subject knowledge and new theories of teaching and learning. I was reading new things on language, and research on language learning, as well as discussing ideas.
>
> (3, partner-teacher)

Both of these comments also remind us of the importance of building and sustaining continuous relationships in what was clearly a research partnership. The Using Computers to Enhance Learning study started with a shared vision of the purposes of the research across the project. This vision was reinforced structurally through the SDTs and the relationships that took it forward were sustained by the continuing interactions between staff from different practices that occurred within them.

These research strategies are not without their challenges for researchers. The aide-memoire for co-construction of research discussed earlier indicates just how important ground rules and shared expectations are. But even then the valuable contributions to practice of an action research-based study can cause problems of its own. In the seminar series, we heard accounts from exhausted researchers of how the professional and curriculum development aspects of what had been planned as nicely contained studies were so successful that the research projects spread like wildfire across schools, with concomitant demands on the research teams. We discuss the importance of project management in almost every chapter in this book and for good reason.

Design experiments and didactical design

An even closer connection with Nissen's idea of prototypes is to be found in the intensive partnerships between researchers and teachers that mark the design experiment approach to developing understandings of pedagogy in specific areas of the school curriculum. Originating in the work of Brown (1992) and Collins (1992), design experiments were initially developed as a kind of formative research to test and refine pedagogic designs, while starting with ideas developed through research on teaching and learning. Cobb *et al.* (2003) describe the purpose of work in this tradition as follows:

> Design experiments are conducted to develop theories, not merely to empirically tune 'what works'. These theories are relatively humble in that they target domain – specific learning processes. For example, a number of research groups working in a domain such as geometry or statistics might collectively develop a design theory that is concerned with the students' learning of key disciplinary ideas in that domain. A theory of this type would specify successive patterns in students' reasoning together with the substantiated means by which the emergence of those successive patterns can be supported.
>
> (9)

Explaining that design experiments aim at addressing the complexity of what they term the 'learning ecology' of classrooms or other instructional settings, Cobb and his colleagues outline a range of approaches to the research partnerships that fall under this label and then identify five common features of these designs. These features are summarized as follows:

- The theories that are produced aim at supporting learning.
- The methodology is interventionist and the studies are often test beds for innovation.

- The studies are both, (i) prospective (implemented to test a hypothesized learning process) and, (ii) reflective (conjecture-driven, with new conjectures arising as the study proceeds).
- The designs are therefore iterative.
- The theories produced must provide guidance for organizing instruction.

There is no blueprint for the actual design of a study of this kind. Indeed, Barab and Squire (2004) describe it not so much as an approach as a series of approaches. Nonetheless, it is useful to see the process as a form of well-documented iterations that start from a firm foundation. It is therefore crucial that the purpose of the study for the researchers and the teachers is clarified at the outset. This is usually done by reviewing previous research to develop a working hypothesis and by examining the student capabilities and current practices in the educational setting. Data collection methods are also selected by both researchers and practitioners and systems for documentation agreed upon.

Cobb *et al.* (2003: 12) acknowledge the demands of such a responsive approach within an experimental framework by emphasizing the need for strong research leadership in four specific areas:

- A clear view of the anticipated learning pathways and potential means of support must be maintained.
- Relationships with practitioners need to be negotiated so that it is seen as a shared enterprise.
- Researchers need to achieve a deep understanding of the ecology of learning as this is a theoretical target for the research.
- Regular debriefing sessions are the forum for reflection and for planning future events. It is in these sessions that the intelligence of the study is generated and communicated.

Reflecting the challenges for researchers in maintaining control over this kind of experimentation, much of the writing on design experiments in the first decade of the twenty-first century has focused on producing a respectable methodology so that the approach can be seen to have legitimacy alongside more established forms of experimentation (e.g. Collins *et al.* 2004). There is therefore the possibility that responsiveness to specific learning ecologies may be downplayed to achieve consistency in approach. Ruthven *et al.*

(2009) have picked up this challenge. Their aim is to contribute to developing what they call

> a public repertoire of theoretically informed tools for [. . .] didactical design: the design of learning environments and teaching sequences informed by close analysis of the specific topic of concern and its framing within a particular subject area.
>
> (329)

Having described a variety of 'theoretically informed tools', they argue that these tools help to 'organize the contributions of grand theories to the processes of designing and evaluating teaching sequences' (340).

Interestingly, when outlining the designs, Ruthven and his colleagues do not question the roles played by the teachers. What the teachers do is simply integrated into the design process and the focus that is shared by the researchers and the teachers is student learning and the systematic gathering of evidence of how it is supported. The different expertise of the researcher-designers and the contextually situated teachers are brought into play in a joint – if managed – enterprise to produce robust and reliable analyses of effective learning environments for students. The aim is therefore not phronesis, though doubtless it can lead to it. Rather, the intention is quite clearly to create what Nissen (2009) describes as prototypes. Though in the writing on design studies there is generally much less attention to Nissen's concern with a continuing questioning of the prototypes that are produced in research partnerships.

Developmental Work Research

DWR is, in its purest form, a distinct research methodology that aims at provoking change in work systems through providing participants in studies with two stimuli: evidence gathered about the everyday practices in their workplaces and the analytic resources with which to question them and reveal the contradictions that are to be found therein. The analytic resources are derived from Marxist and Vygotskian concepts and have been developed by Engeström as 'activity theory'. Engeström's activity theory offers a coherent set of ideas that are translated into the DWR methodology to enable systemic or 'expansive' learning (Engeström 2007, 2008).

In brief, DWR requires researchers to gather evidence about the practices in play in a work setting or across settings. In particular, the researchers focus on what people see as the object of their activity; that is, what it is that they are working on and trying to change. For example, in one TLRP study, which examined how practitioners worked to prevent the social exclusion of young people, the research team found that the object of activity was often a child's trajectory, which practitioners were trying to reconfigure so that the child could connect with what society had to offer them (Edwards *et al.* 2009a).

Data are also gathered from practitioners on the explicit and implicit rules that shape the object of activity, how it can be worked on with the resources available and how the work is shared out. When pulling together a narrative account to present to practitioners for their response in a DWR session, researchers try to bring contradictions to the surface. For example, these may be in the system between two interpretations of the object of activity, or between the object of activity and historically formed rules. Or, the contradiction may arise from features outside the system, for example, amongst the object of activity, the system and that of the wider policy context in which it is located. The contradictions are then presented to all the participants as mirror data to be jointly reflected on in a sequence of two-hour DWR sessions.

In these sessions, participants are led by the researchers to use the analytic resources of activity theory, such as the relationships between tools, rules and the object of activity. The intention is that practitioners recognize the contradictions in their work systems and use the analytic concepts to try to understand them and consequently rethink their practices. Changes in practices and work systems can occur once the object of activity is discussed and worked on by the participants to the extent that it becomes 'expanded'; that is, new possibilities for interpretation and action are revealed. The DWR sessions are recorded and analysed and fed back into subsequent sessions so that understandings of practices are deepened.

One outcome of the process is to reveal new ways of conceptualizing what the practices are doing. In the study of social exclusion this was the main reason for employing DWR. The TLRP Learning in and for Interagency Working (LIW) study aimed at building an understanding of the knowledge that was being created by practitioners as they started to work in new inter-professional ways to support vulnerable children. The practitioners' redefining of the object of their activity, changes in the division of labour and the need to alter the rules that governed their work all gave rise to new ways of thinking about what mattered in their practices – that is, the concepts, such as 'focusing on the whole child', that they used as they did their work. The research team was able to trace these ideas as they developed over sequences of DWR sessions, and to ultimately identify concepts that could be of use more generally to other professionals (Edwards *et al.* 2009a).

The approach connects with both phronesis and the building of prototypes, though because of the emphasis on systemic change cannot be directly equated with either. One important claim for DWR is that it leaves practitioners with the analytic tools of activity theory that are embodied in DWR so that they can continue to interrogate their practices and, for example, responsively adjust rules in order to work on objects of activity as they are being redefined. However, the starting point for these analyses is the system in which the activity is located, reinforcing the need for attention to what Walter *et al.* (2004) have called the 'organizational excellence model' of engagement with research. The scrutiny of practices using DWR methods cannot be done separately from a systemic analysis of organizational purposes. At the same time, how the LIW study used DWR points to a systematic approach to building relatively robust, yet locally sensitive prototypes.

However, it is all too easy for DWR to be something that is done to practitioners and no more than a systematic form of knowledge exchange. Practitioners might benefit from receiving interim analyses of their practices very rapidly in DWR sessions so that they can work with the data while it is still relevant to them, but they may have little control over the intervention itself. The LIW study attempted to overcome this legitimate concern by working relatively intensively with one practitioner-researcher in each setting. These people were senior practitioners who were both members of the research team and responsible for feeding ideas in and out of the study in the local authorities in which they worked. Their role was both pivotal and demanding, and worked best where the local authority had recognized the potential contribution of the study, were receptive to challenges it presented and enabled the collaboration.

Concluding points

In summary, what all of these approaches have in common is the seeking of robust patterns from which some broad principles can

be drawn. To different degrees, they also attempt to engage practitioners in the critical examination of the practices in which they
are located. Let us therefore return to Flyvbjerg (2001) and his
suggestion that social sciences are stronger in an area where the
natural sciences are weak: 'the reflexive analysis and discussion of
values and interests, which is the prerequisite for an enlightened
political, economic, and cultural development of any society' (3).
Chaiklin made a similar point about principles in the closing chapter
of *Understanding Practice*, which he co-edited with Lave:

> There is no expectation that data accumulation alone will be of
> any value. The ultimate aim is to discover or develop general
> principles that can be used to understand specific phenomena.
> (Chaiklin 1993: 383)

We would add that attention to practitioners' engagement in the
research process sharpens that understanding of phenomena in
ways that benefit the practice of research as much as the practices
of education.

We would also argue that the constant and productive interactions across the boundaries of the practice of research and the
various practices that make up education are ethically sound, not
least because they emphasize that research is fed back in timely
ways and that the face validity of ongoing analyses is regularly
checked. These approaches are likely to increase the impact of the
research as our focus on practitioners' engagement in research aims
at ensuring that what matters for both practitioners and researchers
becomes interwoven in the activity of research.

Summary

In this chapter we have outlined why working together in research
can be beneficial for both education-based practitioners and
researchers who work in the area of pedagogy. We have discussed
four research strategies for working with practitioners and have
distinguished between strategies that emphasize knowledge sharing
and those that emphasize co-construction of knowledge. The four
strategies are:

• making knowledge exchange a central feature of research
  design

- building a research study from action research projects
- design experiments and didactical design
- DWR.

As well as bringing knowledge from practice into educational research, all four strategies, in different ways, engage practitioners in the critical examination of the practices in which they are located.

Chapter 4

Engaging service users

This chapter addresses the engagement of service users in and with research. We start by considering who the service users are and what their rationales for engagement in research might be. We then look at various engagement approaches that have been used with school students, adults with disabilities and other kinds of service users. This leads on to discussion of the tensions that can arise in such work, and consideration of lessons learned and ways forward.

Rationale for engaging service users

It is important to clarify what is meant by the term 'service users'. We all make use of some services and service users of research are therefore a very broad group. In this chapter, we are defining service users specifically as the children, adults, students, families or identified groups who may be receiving specialized services (such as looked after children, children with identified special needs, older people), and on which much social science research focuses. However, they are rarely involved in this research, beyond their role as respondents.

There are three main justifications for engaging service users in research. The first is that users across the public services are being encouraged to take greater control over service provision. The second is that there is emerging evidence that service user engagement in the research process may increase the relevance of research. Finally, the involvement of service users throughout the process of research is likely to increase the impact of that research. Each of these reasons is now considered in more detail.

Greater control of public services by users

Within education, the speech by Miliband (2004) at the North of England Education Conference, though by no means the first discussion of personalized learning, elevated its status in education in both the policy and practice arenas. Since then, there has been much debate and confusion about the definition, implementation and utility of personalized public services. However, this debate extends well beyond education to the wider public services. In essence, the personalization policy claims that giving individuals and groups greater opportunity to articulate their preferences and choices in public services will enable diverse needs to be met more effectively and achieve greater equality. In *Building Britain's Future* (HM Government 2009), the government set out a programme for empowering people with new entitlements to high-quality education, health care and policing. In 2009, in *Power in People's Hands*, the Cabinet Office Strategy Unit provided the government rationale for greater personalization and empowerment of users in the provision of public services:

> Achieving not merely adequate standards in services, but high-quality, personalised responses to the aspirations of millions of citizens, rests on ensuring that people can better direct services themselves. At the same time, front-line professionals need enhanced freedoms, skills and links to their local communities, in order to respond better to service users.
>
> (8)

No empirical evidence is provided for this assertion (beyond further assertions that emerged from the interviews they conducted with others) that high-quality services can be achieved through greater personalization and the empowerment of users. Foster *et al.* (2006), in a study of frontline practitioners in social care, concluded that their awareness of the constraints and limitations of resources influenced the assessment process and decision-making. These researchers found that frontline practitioners were interpreting and implementing policy into practice, during which they inevitably retained some power, whatever the organizational and policy intentions set out by the personalization agenda.

Leadbeater (2004) distinguished between 'deep personalization' and 'shallow personalization'. In deep personalization, professionals are brokers of services helping clients generate pathways through the available range of provision that meet their particular needs. In contrast, shallow personalization simply involves the service providers acting more efficiently to meet specific individual needs, without the direct involvement of the consumer. Campbell *et al.* (2007) suggest that, as long as the state maintains control of the finances for delivering the services, deep personalization will remain at a rhetorical level. Drawing on data from their research with students identified as gifted and talented, they conclude their critique of personalization by noting that:

> [i]t is easier to implement reforms that merely increase system efficiency, but much more difficult to implement the 'disruptive' innovation in role relationships between teacher and learner, envisaged by deep personalisation in Leadbeater's terms. In the end, what Leadbeater is arguing for is a radical change in the control of educational knowledge production.
>
> (153)

They note that the control of knowledge production as expounded in the curriculum, pedagogy and assessment, has not been something that recent governments have been willing to hand over.

Despite the critiques of personalized services and of their capacity to achieve better quality, there has been an increase in attempts to empower users throughout the public services and recognition of the changes that this implies for staff and management. The quotation above from Campbell *et al.* (2007) acknowledges the additional demands that this implies for frontline professionals, in terms of support to develop the capacity to respond to service users. The increase in personalization provides a broader and important context for considering service users' engagement in research. In a climate in which service users are being encouraged to take greater control over the services they receive, there should be an increased expectation for greater involvement in the research that focuses on their services.

Service users increase the relevance of research

The second main reason for engaging service users in research is to ensure greater relevance of research. Relevance can be increased by engaging service users throughout the process from the initial ideas and formulation of a research question, through the process of data collection and analysis, to the verification of alternative interpretations or explanations of the findings. In the ESRC seminar series, Barnes presented a cogent argument for recognizing the political and epistemological assumptions underlying research with mental health service users which she identified in her research as 'knowledge being best generated *with* people' and 'taking part in research is empowering' (Barnes 2006). The service user has first-hand experience of the service that is the focus of the research. The researcher, service manager or policy-maker may think that they have identified the issues from previous research, evaluation of outcomes or policy needs, but these may not reflect the perspectives of the service user themselves. Furthermore, the importance and priority ascribed to specific issues may be different for those experiencing the service provision.

Involving service users from the start of the research process can identify different priorities that might influence the research design. In a recent evaluation of UNICEF UK's Rights Respecting Schools Award (Sebba and Robinson 2010), the evaluation team sought advice from two school leavers from a school involved in the programme, about both the focus of the research questions and the data collection methods. The students were adamant that the key effects of the scheme would be more evident outside formal lessons, a perspective that influenced the data collection (to incorporate playground and lunchtime observations) and the interview questions to parents, pupils and school staff. The data that subsequently emerged from different respondents were sometimes contradictory, providing strong confirmation of the wisdom of acting upon these two service users' input.

Service users increase the impact of research

A third justification for engaging service users concerns the increase in the impact of research that can be achieved through engaging service users throughout the process. As Barnes and Taylor, in their helpful guide to involving older people in research, suggest:

> The involvement of research users is emphasized not only to ensure the relevance of the topics and approaches adopted, but also to maximize the likelihood that research findings will have an impact. It suggests that 'user groups' should have a role

in translating findings into more understandable and policy relevant recommendations and that they should be funded to enable them to play this role.

(2007: 6)

They go on to provide examples of research that adopt a range of approaches to involving older people, some of which are referred to later in this chapter. Barnes and Taylor note that a key difference between research that accesses people's understandings and interpretations of their lives and that which is participatory or emancipatory, is that the latter seeks explicitly to lead to change that liberates the service users.

Undertaking research in public services is inevitably messy. Carefully constructed research designs become threatened by practical challenges such as the availability of those in the sample, changes in policy influencing provision and variations in the definitions or measurement of supposedly standard measures (e.g. school attendance rates). Changes to the research design are common and often the subject of negotiation with the professionals and service users involved. Discussions and questions posed during the data collection inevitably have an impact on the service itself. In this sense, much research in public services draws on aspects of action research in that it is impacting on the service during the research process. Increasing involvement of service users in the research process is thereby likely to lead to ongoing impact of the research on the service. Barnes and Taylor (2007) argue that service users are claiming a more active role in the research that affects them because they have sometimes felt exploited by research that treats them as objects and fails to improve their lives. It is important to acknowledge that impact is not always a positive experience (for example, when research suggests that a service is poor value for money and thereby leads to its reduction or withdrawal).

Finally, involving service users in research develops capacity in the system. Involving people in research who are not researchers enables them to learn the potential value of research and some research skills. It also encourages them to draw on skills (e.g. interviewing) that were learned in another context that might be valued in a research context, thus enhancing the self-esteem of the service user.

Approaches to engaging service users in research

Research on engaging service users focuses on a range of users – for example, students, older people and people with mental health issues – and a variety of approaches to involvement in the research. Barnes and Taylor (2007) note that older people have been engaged as research practitioners, advisors, commissioners, direct users, campaigners and active subjects of research.

Involving students in research

Unsurprisingly, in the educational sphere, service user engagement in research has focused mainly on school students. Punch (2002) noted the danger of children being marginalized in an adult-centred society and suggested that participatory research methods were helpful in partly addressing this. Research projects in which young people have been involved in the design or conduct of the research (as opposed to the larger number of studies that have sought the views of children and young people) are relatively recent and few in number. One of the most influential of these attempts was the work undertaken by Fielding and Bragg. In 2001, Fielding published 'Students as radical agents of change', in which he argued for an approach that avoids unintentional manipulation of students in favour of facilitating them to become transformational leaders. In the context of a performative culture, he contended that students can too often be used to collect data in order to meet accountability requirements, rather than being engaged in the research process as an educative exercise in itself. In the approach taken by Fielding and the staff of one secondary school, collective control was invested in a group of students of mixed age, gender and attainment who were trained in research methods. The students identified issues that they saw as priorities in the school and then collected data with the support of staff, in order to clarify the nature of the issue and make recommendations for addressing it. In at least two areas researched in the first year – that of student profiling and training and support for the school council – the recommendations were acted upon immediately by the management.

The student researchers at this school ran workshops at which they presented their ongoing work at professional development days and staff meetings. In sharing their emerging research findings, they sought to engage staff in discussions of issues, problems and progress, and as such these events provided opportunities for genuine co-production of new knowledge. The work on students as researchers expanded extensively at this school and beyond, with involvement in other schools to encourage and support similar initiatives. However, as Thomson and Gunter (2006) have noted, working with students as researchers requires an ongoing process of negotiation, which acknowledges the possibility of being simultaneously oppressive and transformative.

Fielding and Bragg (2003) went on to provide practical support materials for developing the engagement of students in research, drawing on their experience from the ESRC TLRP-funded The ESRC Network Project: Consulting Pupils about Teaching and Learning. These support materials include examples of students undertaking research into learning and into the conditions that support it, evidence of the impact of their work, and guidance about ways of providing basic training in research.

The ESRC Network Project: Consulting Pupils about Teaching and Learning (http://www.consultingpupils.co.uk) was co-led by the late Jean Rudduck, one of the two great thinkers in this field to whom this book is dedicated. Rudduck herself undertook a series of studies on pupil involvement and personalized learning in which she demonstrated the value of engaging students in research. For example, in her account of a personalized learning project she notes that:

> students also took responsibility for aspects of the research and development themselves: they designed and analyzed questionnaires for finding out what their peers – and in one case their peers' parents – thought about the agreed issues; they formed groups to follow up the concerns that their peers had raised in initial interviews; they collated and analyzed the data they had gathered and presented reports to the senior management team or to heads of department/subject meetings.
>
> (Rudduck *et al.* 2005: 4)

The evidence from these studies of students as researchers suggest that service users undertaking research, such as interviewing other users of the same service, may generate more authentic data. Jacklin *et al.* (2007) examined the experiences of disabled students in one university and how these could be improved. Student co-researchers were self-selected, when being interviewed in an earlier stage of the project, by expressing an interest in becoming involved. The researchers began with a focus group of 14 students using a nominal group technique to gain an in-depth understanding and greater critical edge on emerging findings. A core group of seven students then became co-researchers, identifying issues seen as important to the students, conducting interviews with each other on their experiences as disabled students, collecting visual illustrations of some of the issues identified and disseminating the research findings. These co-researchers identified five key issues in the findings and developed associated recommendations for policymakers and higher education institutions. While this example stops short of the students controlling the research completely, it meets Barnes and Taylor's (2007) criterion for emancipatory research in enabling the disabled students to use research to improve their service provision.

Involving adults with disabilities and mental health issues in research

The research on the social context of disability by Shakespeare (e.g. 1993) has been seminal in challenging orthodoxy by documenting the powerlessness and objectification of disabled people, though he argued that this was insufficiently conceptualized by social movement theory.

Dowse (2009) draws on collaborative action research (CAR) based on critical reflection with two self-advocacy groups of people with learning disabilities, in England and Australia, to argue for emancipatory research controlled by disabled people, rather than simply involving them in the research process. Her position is similar to that of Barnes and Taylor (2007), in suggesting that such research can lead to co-constructed forms of knowledge and research agendas. She argues that a reflexive and collaborative research design must be adopted to achieve this. People with learning disabilities in her study became aware that research can address questions of relevance to their lives. She noted that identifying a problem in their lives that needed to be addressed, reconsidering the conditions that create or sustain the problem and discussing possible solutions enabled the people with learning disabilities to engage in the research. The researcher's role becomes that of a change catalyst or facilitator, empowering the service user to change.

In Chapter 2, we illustrated user-led research with the example of the Suresearch network of mental health service users as researchers in projects undertaken at the University of Birmingham. Members of Suresearch are full members of research teams, undertaking fieldwork and contributing to analyses, and have gradually developed research skills over time through sustained involvement in research. They also communicate research outcomes in ways that clearly identify the potential impact of the findings.

In Chapter 3 we discussed Theories of Change (Connell and Kubisch 1998) as a key example of an evaluation design that privileges knowledge-sharing. It requires researchers to identify and respond to the theories of change held by different stakeholders in an initiative. As such, the strategy has been described as 'co-research' in a way that supports Barnes and Taylor (2007), Dowse (2009), Suresearch and our own position throughout this book that relationships between researchers and users enable the unique skills and experiences of each to be mutually beneficial. Two-way interchange is emphasized, to which researchers bring knowledge and expertise from their research and service users from their experience of the service.

The approach Dowse took to the research was guided by her determination to establish authentic service user engagement in it. She adopted mixed methods including ethnography, narrative, observation, participation and dialogue. The focus of the research emerged in response to ways to improve the organization (an advocacy group) and lives of the participants. To ensure access for the participants, researchers minimized concepts and ideas and avoided jargon, while at the same time actively listened, even when participant communications were unclear. She noted that the main ideas needed to be summarized regularly in plain English and discussed until the participants were satisfied that their true feelings and experiences were being accurately represented. She argued that engaging with the users in the context of their own practices (here, self-advocacy) offered insights that could expand our understanding of the issues (in this case, social relations of disability). Dowse (2009: 150) concludes:

> The approach therefore offers a new tool for disability scholarship as a discipline to broaden its engagement with the range of experiences of disablement grounded in the voices and experiences of those it seeks to study.

Involving service users in systematic reviewing

The only reported study of school students in systematic reviewing to date is of the Hatch End School students who led a systematic review on school programmes that encourage conflict resolution and peer mediation (Garcia *et al.* 2006). The review group was made up of a team of nine students (in Years 10 and 11), five teachers and a parent, with an advisory group composed of academics and other researchers in the field of relationships education. The Year 10 students who agreed to take part were an already established group that had previously been involved in local authority-wide initiatives in personal, social and health education (PSHE) and sex and relationships education (SRE). The review question was: *Do planned educational interventions in conflict resolution skills, negotiation skills and peer mediation, improve young people's personal and social relationships?* This was chosen by the students and teachers. The students had input to the inclusion and exclusion criteria that were applied to the initial screening of the abstracts and to the identification of the 12 studies included the in-depth analysis. In addition, they provided perspectives on the interpretation of the findings from the synthesis. In parallel to the review, the students undertook primary research in the school using questionnaires and interviews to determine the views of the students about young people's personal and social relationships and how this was addressed in the curriculum of the school.

Braye and Preston-Shoot (2005, see also the seminar papers on the TLRP website http://www.tlrp.org/themes/seminar/edwards/current.html), describe a specific type of participatory research in the form of the engagement of adult service users in systematic reviewing. They developed a way of undertaking systematic reviews that incorporated non-research-based evidence in the form of the testimonies of 'experts by experience' (such as service users and carers). They saw this as challenging the epistemological assumptions of traditional systematic reviewing methodology since, drawing on Pawson (2003), they noted that it involves using a wider range of sources including research, policy documentation, practice and users' experience. The approach they used when involving service users also differs from traditional systematic reviewing, in that extracted and synthesized data from qualitative, non-experimental and even non-research sources were included. While much systematic reviewing in education and social work has moved beyond the limits of experimental studies (see, for example, Sharland and Taylor 2006; Barnett-Page and Thomas 2009), the inclusion criteria usually stop short of including some of the non-research sources that Braye and Preston-Shoot suggest are assessed using fitness for purpose criteria.

Braye and Preston-Shoot used stakeholder conferences as the main strategy for working with service users and carers, as they argue that these offer commonality and support. They drew on group work theory, which informed the composition, stages of development, task and process balance, dynamics of power and influence, and structured techniques to facilitate participation. The stakeholder conferences took place alongside the reviewing of international research and a national survey of practice, and were seen to provide a reference group proactively steering the research and interpretation of data.

Tensions in engaging service users

In the ESRC seminar series, several participants raised tensions in the competing demands on researchers to develop authentic service user engagement while meeting academic quality standards and funding deadlines. They acknowledged the time and effort needed to genuinely engage service users, time that is rarely reflected in the contracts issued by research funders. Dowse (2009: 143) notes the dilemma of

> how to do research in intellectual disability that is grounded in and guided by the views and interests of such people themselves, while at the same time meeting the criteria of academic institutions or funding bodies for scholarly rigor and accountability.

Dowse goes on to suggest that ideas and concepts need to be pared down to the minimum to provide access to the research process for the service users (people with learning disabilities, in her study). While she suggests that this can be arduous, she also considers it to be liberating for the researcher. Some might argue, though, that for researchers, complex relationships and theories cannot be reduced to short, sharp messages without losing research integrity.

A further tension for the researcher, identified by Dowse and others, is the competing power exerted on them from different sources, influences that come simultaneously from funding bodies and from the oppositional traditions and expectations of the academy, and in the case of Dowse's research, from the disability movement. In the context of personalized public services, there is a potential tension in the power relationship between frontline practitioner and service user, which might influence the capacity of service users to become engaged in research. Webb (2008) has warned against service user participation that becomes unconscious collusion, or appears to agree, with the service providers, researchers or others because of this power differential. He also noted that it had become a 'mantra' or 'mission' in some contexts, making careful evaluation critical to distinguishing between genuine process and zeal.

Barnes and Taylor (2007; Barnes 2008) argue that service user engagement in research should be emancipatory, the impact of the research improving the service provided. However, this requires frontline practitioners to facilitate service users' involvement by relinquishing some of their decision-making power. In both Dowse's (2009) study and Foster et al.'s (2006) research on the assessment process, this presents considerable challenges when the service user has disabilities that limit communication. The researcher is thereby faced with the need to establish effective channels for the service user to contribute, while handling the 'gatekeeper' practitioners sensitively.

In Lencucha et al.'s (2010) systematic review of community-based participatory research, 42 studies in health care were synthesized to develop a knowledge transfer triad framework amongst community groups, researchers and decision-makers. Within this, the review identified the structures, principles, processes and relationships that seem to be effective in addressing the tensions identified above. Lencucha et al. provide guidance on how to incorporate community stakeholder groups in genuine collaboration and the key elements that can facilitate collaboration amongst researchers, decision-makers and community groups, emphasizing the reciprocity rather than the linearity of their relationships. They note that decision-makers are more likely to be influenced by presentation of evidence-informed arguments from community groups than by a lone researcher.

Lessons learned and ways forward

The examples of service user engagement in research reviewed in this chapter provide approaches to engaging service users in research alongside beliefs about knowledge, its production and its use. They have also provided clear warnings of the dangers of unintended manipulation, exploitation or tokenism. Where the research is genuinely emancipatory, these dangers have been avoided. Some of the specific approaches that have contributed to this emerge clearly from the examples.

First, in all the accounts that effectively engage service users, the involvement has started from the outset of the research, in the identification of the problem or issue to be addressed that has been formulated into a research question. Second, while retaining researcher expertise, the research process has been fully discussed with service users who have been invited to contribute to decisions about how to progress. Third, these effective initiatives have handled the gatekeeper role (performed by parents, teachers, other frontline professionals) sensitively. This might involve negotiations with gatekeepers who are fully supportive or have initiated the service user engagement themselves. Since service user engagement more often takes place in the context of research that focuses on the service, the gatekeeper might feel threatened that their care, practice or authority could be challenged by the emerging findings. Over time, sustained engagement often leads to greater acceptance of the value of users engaged in enquiries about the service, in ways that bring about positive change.

Fourth, the challenge to researchers of needing to ensure that all communication is clear and concise, while maintaining academic rigour, is welcomed in a climate in which greater emphasis is being placed, by both funders and research assessors, on the impact of research. Finally, the examples illustrate the benefits of service user engagement in building capacity in the system to undertake research in a wide variety of settings that can lead to transformational change.

Summary

This chapter has considered the engagement of service users in research. The rationale for engaging service users in research that was set out at the start of the chapter emphasized the increasing personalization of public services, which claims to give greater control to service users. Further justification for engaging service users in research was provided by describing its potential for increasing both the relevance and impact of research. Examples of ways in which service users have been engaged in research were described. The tensions, in particular for the researcher, in engaging service users were discussed and some lessons noted. Overall, the illustrations of effective service user engagement demonstrate that, while major challenges need to be acknowledged and addressed, the potential for improving research through engaging service users is considerable.

Chapter 5

Engaging policy-makers

In this chapter we consider the ways in which policy-makers can be engaged in and with research. After defining who we are referring to as policy-makers, we explore what is known about the policy-making process and how research can be used effectively within it, illustrating this with examples. The ways in which engaging policy-makers in research processes can improve the use of research is discussed. Finally, we consider the lessons learned and implications for future development.

Background

Research on whether, and how, policy-makers use research to inform their decisions is not new. Over 30 years ago, Weiss (1980), in a seminal paper, reported research undertaken at Columbia University on policy-makers' perceptions of their use of research. She noted that amongst 155 high-level officials interviewed in federal, state and local mental health agencies, the majority claimed to use research, though most not consciously. Weiss suggested that research fills in the background for the officials, supplying the context from which they derive ideas, concepts and policy options. She concluded that

> [s]ocial science, by helping to structure people's perceptions of social reality, seems to have pervasive effects. It provides an underlying set of ideas, models of the interaction of people, conditions, and events, which enter into our images of how the world works. The respondents in our study underscored this indirect kind of knowledge creep.

(397)

There is very little empirical research on the wider issues of whether, and if so how, research impacts on policy in education, or indeed in other areas (for example, in health care, which is often held up to be more advanced in the use of research; e.g. Tetroe *et al.* 2008). Within this small evidence base, there is a dearth of empirical research on user engagement in the research process. Researchers of the use of evidence in policy making (e.g. S. Campbell *et al.* 2007; Innvaer *et al.* 2002; Levin 2004b, 2008; Lomas *et al.* 2005; Rigby 2005; Rich 2004) suggest, as noted on pp. 84–5, that policy makers favour other sources of evidence over research. Nutley *et al.* (2007) and Levin (2008) both acknowledge that the focus for research impact has been on the individual, rather than at the organizational or system level.

The processes that operate in the use of research in practice need to be distinguished from those that function in relation to policy-making. However, in particular from 1997 in England, national education policy has been characterized by the production and distribution of guidance on practice in a wide range of areas (e.g. assessment, literacy, behaviour, attendance, special educational needs, school management, etc.). Alongside these extensive publications, a far-reaching network of trainers (sometimes referred to as the 'field-force'), has been appointed to support and monitor the implementation of these strategies. This apparent micro-managing of local practice in schools by the central administration, defines a somewhat different relationship between policy and practice than hitherto existed. In this context, research findings that influence policy, and are therefore reflected, albeit implicitly, in the training materials and activities of these national strategies, are thus likely to be discernible in classroom practice. Hence, there will be some overlap between the research evident in policy and that reflected in practice, in a system within which much national policy translates into directives on classroom practice.

In Chapter 1, we explored the many possible interpretations of the term 'research users'. As a subset of these research users, policy-makers might include politicians, civil servants (more usually referred to as administrators outside England); government agencies; regional, local and district politicians; and regulatory bodies (such as those setting standards or inspecting practice). The seminar discussions concluded that the term 'decision-maker' might sometimes be more helpful than 'user' because of its focus on helping people to make better decisions and its capacity to include groups such as students and parents as well as teachers and civil servants.

Furthermore, there are researchers and research analysts working inside government who might be referred to as 'insider-researchers' (Brown 2009) but who, while not directly responsible for policy, might be expected to have greater influence on policy decisions than do external researchers. The challenge of identifying exactly *who* makes policy links to our discussion of the challenges in identifying *how* policy is made. Nutley suggested in the seminars (see also Figure 5.1, p. 80) that political advisors should be seen as policy-makers alongside politicians and civil servants. In addition to those involved in policy-making centrally, there are local politicians in councils, districts or provinces involved in both generating policy for their local area and translating national policy in the local context.

The urgency of the need to focus on research use in policy arises from the frustration of researchers who consider that their findings should but do not make a difference; and of policy-makers who want clear, unequivocal 'messages' that provide the basis for policy options. This apparent divergence in views of the function of research is further explored in this chapter. More fundamentally, as Oakley (2000: 3) has suggested,

> [t]he goal of an emancipatory (social) science calls for us to abandon sterile word-games and concentrate on the business in hand, which is how to develop the most reliable and democratic ways of knowing, both in order to bridge the gap between ourselves and others, and *to ensure that those who intervene in other people's lives do so with the most benefit and the least harm.* [emphasis added]

Since, in education, both policy-makers and practitioners (through national policy implementation and in their own right) intervene in the lives of others on a daily basis, the use of evidence to inform this process would seem to be a moral requirement rather than a matter of debate. Nevertheless, whose evidence, what constitutes evidence and how it should be used, are understandably all contested areas.

Research in the policy process

In the conclusions of the seminar series it was suggested that research-based knowledge can interrupt practice, and practice has the potential to interrupt taken-for-granted aspects of research. This is helpful since it enables each one to inform the other, drawing on specific experience and expertise. The same may apply to policy. Research-based knowledge can interrupt the policy-making process by challenging assumptions, suggesting additional options, presenting alternative interpretations or confirming existing judgements. Policy-making can interrupt the research process by challenging the relevancy of the research question, suggesting alternative ways of accessing data from public services, presenting alternative interpretations or requesting an alternative timescale. To maximize the benefits that might accrue from these interactions, we need to create ways of generating these interruptions.

The assumption held by many researchers is that there is a linear relationship between research and policy – researchers report the findings, and politicians and civil servants use them to make decisions. Hence, when this relationship is lacking, there are increasing tensions and frustration between the researchers and policy-makers. Many writers (e.g. Levin 2004b, 2008; Nutley *et al.* 2007) have provided rich analyses of the policy process demonstrating that this linear relationship does not hold and proposing non-linear explanatory models.

Lomas (1993) categorized knowledge translation activities into three types: *diffusion*, which is essentially passive and unplanned, leaving the user to seek out the information; *dissemination*, which is an active process of communication of the findings that involves customizing the evidence for a particular target audience; and *implementation*, which is a more active process that involves systematic efforts to encourage adoption of the evidence. Diffusion and dissemination can raise awareness and might influence attitudes, but are unlikely to change the behaviour, whereas implementation strategies, in particular when they include addressing any barriers, have a better chance of doing so.

Lavis *et al.* (2003) proposed an alternative model of knowledge translation based on the degree of engagement with potential users. Activities are categorized as producer *push*, which disseminate or 'push out' the information and hope that users receive and use it; user *pull*, which focuses on the needs of users, thereby creating a demand for the findings; and *linkage and exchange,* which are about developing networks and relationships in order to exchange knowledge and ideas. Amara *et al.* (2004) note that the more intense the interactions between users and researchers, the more likely it is that the research will be used. Linkage mechanisms are the means by which this intensity can be measured and can include activities such as meetings, conferences, scientific seminars and communication by email or through the internet.

The model of knowledge transfer proposed by Nutley (see Figure 5.1) at the second seminar in our ESRC series shows the policy-makers as the politicians, civil servants and political advisors. The extensive but undocumented (except in memoirs) influence of political advisors in decision-making should not be underestimated. Nutley identifies a range of 'knowledge brokers', or 'intermediaries', who, through a variety of means (e.g. direct contact, media coverage, written summaries), 'translate' the work of researchers into short accessible sound bites for busy policy-makers. In so doing, however, these organizations, or in some cases individuals (e.g. 'experts' who may or may not be drawing on an evidence base), have the opportunity to slant the findings to suit their particular perspectives or needs. Lobby groups provide explicit examples of this. One think tank – Demos, whose previous director Tom Bentley contributed to the seminars – developed a distinctive approach to research that involved working in partnership with public, private and voluntary sector partners. Demos saw its role as increasing the

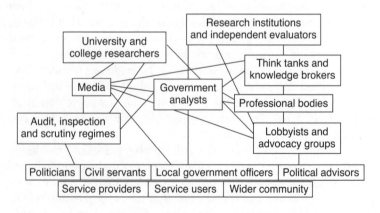

Figure 5.1 The many active players in policy networks (Nutley 2005)

engagement of users in policy-orientated research through acting either as an intermediary or in collaboration on research with other organizations.

The process is not linear for a number of reasons. Research on policy makers' attitudes towards research (e.g. S. Campbell *et al.* 2007; Kirst 2000; Lomas *et al.* 2005; Rigby 2005) concludes that policy-makers often regard research findings as ambiguous, conflicting, insignificant, untimely or only partially relevant. Lomas *et al.*, in undertaking a systematic review of the literature on how the concept of evidence is treated in health care, distinguished three categories of evidence:

> medical effectiveness research (context-free scientific evidence); social science-oriented research (context sensitive scientific evidence); or the expertise, views, and realities of stakeholders (colloquial evidence). These views of evidence are not incompatible and each has a role to play in producing evidence-based guidance . . .
>
> (2005: 5)

They noted that decision-makers view evidence colloquially and define it by its relevance. In contrast, researchers tend to view evidence scientifically (i.e. by the use of systematic, replicable methods or robust qualitative analysis through triangulation) and define it by its methodology. Hence, there are well-established differences in the culture of how evidence is viewed. Lomas *et al.* go on to suggest that 'deliberative processes' can be used effectively to combine these different approaches with representation from both the scientific and stakeholder communities, leading to 'guidance that respects both scientific integrity on the one hand and its implementability in a specific health system context on the other' (5). A deliberative process is distinguished from a consultative process as being characterized by much more extensive participation. It is also transparent, explicit, inclusive and has clear objectives. Thus, systematic reviewing in social sciences that involves users would seem to constitute a 'deliberative process', though Lomas *et al.* (2005), working in the context of health care, categorize systematic reviewing as a 'scientific' activity whereas deliberative processes, in their view, bring together all kinds of evidence. The forms of systematic reviewing that have developed in the UK through the EPPI centre (www.eppi.ac.uk) and the Social Care Institute for

Excellence (www.scie.org.uk) over the last ten years, have similarly involved combining all types of evidence and so might be regarded as deliberative processes.

Effective engagement of policy-makers in research

Research is most likely to be used in policy if policy-makers have been involved in its development (Lomas *et al.* 2005). Research produces knowledge that can be applied, and the involvement of users in the research process can lead to a stronger alignment between the priorities of policy-makers and researchers and the perception of policy-makers that the research is of greater relevance (Nutley *et al.* 2007). The receptivity of potential research users to research outputs is critical. Where they have been involved from the outset, as, for example, some local authority senior managers were in the Learning how to Learn TLRP project (http://www.learntolearn. ac.uk/), in influencing the focus of the research, some data collection, interpretation of emerging findings and verification of the conclusions, receptivity to the outcomes was high.

The analysis of TLRP projects and research networks undertaken during the seminar series suggested that there were particular stages of the research in which users (in the analysis this included policy-makers and practitioners) were more likely to be involved. These included developing research instruments (for example, by contributing to discussions about questions to include in interviews); data collection (for example, by accessing data on characteristics of schools); verifying interpretations of data; disseminating findings, insights and ideas; and suggesting implications for action. In the main, users were not involved in writing the research proposal, though they often influenced the research questions. Neither were they generally involved in data analysis. Some outputs from the programme were co-authored with practitioners or policy makers and the user engagement appears to have been genuine rather than tokenistic.

The wider literature highlights five factors as influential upon policy-makers' engagement in research. These include the nature of the research, characteristics of policy-makers, mediators and brokers, timing, and personal factors.

Nature of the research

Certain characteristics of the research may influence whether policy-makers are likely to take notice of it. Landry *et al.* (2001), in a survey of over 1,200 academic social scientists about the extent of research use, noted that

> the most important finding of this paper is that knowledge utilization depends much more heavily on factors related to the behavior of the researchers' and users' context than on the attributes of the research products.
>
> (347)

Despite Landry *et al.*'s and others' conclusions on the limited impact of the research products themselves, there is evidence from the TLRP programme and associated research projects (e.g. Effective Pre-School and Primary Education 3–11 [EPPE] Project longitudinal study, which has been very influential on policy and practice) that research that is longitudinal, integrates quantitative and qualitative data and focuses on an area of current policy concern (which applies to most government-sponsored research) will receive policy attention. Policy-makers require research to be presented in ways that are jargon-free, succinct and give concrete illustrations. So researchers need to use and communicate their expertise in new ways.

> An important aspect of all this is the ability to respond when the information is needed and to apply knowledge flexibly to novel situations, rather than reiterating past nostrums.
>
> (Commission on the Social Sciences 2003: 70)

The EPPE project provides a good example of this and more details are available in Sylva *et al.* (2007). This longitudinal study began in 1996 and followed through a cohort of infants to assess the effects of different preschool and, later, primary school experiences. The findings noted that the quality of provision and length of time that children were enrolled in early years education made a major and sustained contribution to children's later progress and attainment. These findings were subsequently reflected in policy, which Sylva *et al.* attribute to researchers establishing an early and continuing close working relationship with policy-makers.

Many researchers assume (e.g. Whitty 2002) that policy-makers are not interested in blue skies research as it rarely relates to current policy. However, some policy-makers (e.g. Brown 2009; DCSF 2008) claim that research that advances ideas, rather than evaluating current policy implementation, is needed to inform future policy options. The seminar discussion concluded that researchers need to think more about sharing ideas and concepts and policy-makers need to see researchers as sources of ideas. This raises interesting questions concerning the role of research in generating ideas and the role of ideas in developing research evidence.

Characteristics of policy-makers

Kirst (2000: 386) identified the characteristics of policy makers that affect their receptivity to information as:

- Motivation to seek and use information.
- Resistance to outside sources or innovative suggestions.
- Sense of ownership of, or commitment to use particular information.
- Responsibilities for existing and incompatible policies.
- Insufficient resources.
- Fragmented authority to act.
- Competing or conflicting demands on institutional resources.

Thus, policy-makers have many other factors to take into account, including political (e.g. party policy, public opinion, stakeholder groups), economic, timing and assessment of likely outcomes.

Rigby's (2005) research with 14 individuals who work within the federal policy-making process in the US and who could be regarded as research mediators or knowledge brokers, noted that policy-makers filter research through the value-laden lens of political discourse. Further, she concluded that policy-makers rely primarily on three sources of information: commissions, gurus and think tanks, with social science researchers working in academe rarely consulted, though researchers working within government were reported to be much more influential. S. Campbell *et al.* (2007) held interviews and group discussions with 42 policy-makers in England, in a range of middle management and senior civil service positions and, similarly to Rigby, found that academic researchers did not rate highly in the type of evidence prioritized by policy makers.

Kirst (2000) suggested that, from the policy-makers' perspective, information can be viewed as an asset, a liability, or as simply irrelevant. Using any information is, as John Maynard Keynes pointed out, more work for the policy-maker: 'There is nothing a politician likes so little as to be well informed; it makes decision-making so complex and difficult' (cited in Davis *et al.* 1999).

Chapman (2002), in a booklet published by the think tank Demos, about the importance of using systems analysis in policy-making, suggests that the civil service in England is judged by failure. It is this, he states, that leads to the inevitable distortion of information at every level because no one wishes to communicate bad news or to expose themselves to blame. The modernizing government agenda in England began to challenge this culture, though bringing about this change is slow and hard and there are few incentives to complicate the task of policy-making further by grappling with unclear messages from research.

Mediators and brokers

Knowledge is mediated through third parties such as lobby groups, the media and think tanks (Levin 2004a). Rarely are researchers in direct contact with policy-makers. As we have seen, Campbell, S. *et al.* (2007) and Rigby (2005) reported that senior officials and politicians privilege contact with commissions, 'experts' and think tanks over researchers as sources of information. Research is mediated by many individuals and groups, including researchers, funders, teacher educators, education officers and policy analysts. 'Research mediators' and 'think tanks' are terms used in the literature to describe individuals, groups, organizations and even processes (such as a 'commission') that make research and practice, or research and policy-making, more accessible to one another (Ward *et al.* 2009).

Research mediators work at the researcher–policy-maker interface. They maintain links with policy networks; translate research reports into accessible language, oral policy briefings or media presentations; and synthesize findings from a range of sources (Kirst 2000). Specifically, in relation to think tanks, McNutt and Marchildon (2009: 223) suggest that their functions include

problem definition (policy analysis), challenges to existing programs (evaluation), expansion of public debate (community outreach), innovation (policy research), and knowledge broker-age (collaboration).

Examples emerge from the literature of ways in which research mediation can work effectively. The New South Wales Department of Health and the Sax Institute have developed a knowledge bro-kering system that includes a commissioning tool for specifying the requirements of an evidence review, a register of experienced researchers to carry out the review and a dedicated individual to liaise between policy-makers and researchers during the commis-sioning process (Martinez and Campbell 2007, cited in Ward *et al.* 2009: 370).

However, research mediation should be critically considered. Rich's (2004) findings that those working for think tanks in the US came from media or political backgrounds rather than policy or research raises major concerns about the privileging of information from think tanks. Haas' (2007) contention that think tanks often present themselves as researchers, despite their lack of research experience (Rich 2004) and while not subjecting their findings to peer review, should be of concern to the research community and confirms the picture presented by Ball and Exley (2010). The influence of think tanks is often assessed by media exposure, publications produced or number of invitations to speak to par-liamentary committees, but as Abelson (2007) has noted, these are measures of exposure, not influence. Hence, while research mediators are ever-increasingly key players in enhancing policy-makers engagement with research, the benefits of this need critical consideration.

The role played by quasi-researchers within government, govern-ment agencies, non-departmental public bodies and the voluntary sector (who are in some cases researchers and policy-makers) is different from that of researchers working in higher education or within private research consultancies. Brown (2009) refers to the former group as 'insider researchers' and, having worked within a non-departmental public body (otherwise referred to as a 'quango') himself, he notes the greater direct access that these insider-researchers may have to ministers and senior officials compared with the 'outsider-researchers' from the higher education or independent sectors. This relatively strong influence of insider-researchers was a key conclusion in Rigby's (2005) study.

Timing

Emerging from the seminars was strong agreement that questions of timing, timescales and time were central to all activities associated with working with users. A major challenge for researchers is judging when to make contact with policy-makers in terms of identifying emerging priority issues: whether to wait for the moment when a senior policy person is looking for particular information or to get involved when ideas are in development, for example, through policy task forces.

The diverging timescales of policy, practice and research are an ongoing challenge. Alan Dyson (in the seminar discussion) saw this in terms of an inevitable tension between acting and understanding, and quoted Søren Kierkegaard, the Danish philosopher: 'It is perfectly true, as philosophers say, that life must be understood backwards. But they forget the other proposition, that it must be lived forwards' (quoted in Gardiner 1988: 127). In other words, there is always a mismatch between what we know and what we want to know. There are, however, some strategies for addressing the divergence of timescales between research and policy. Developing a better and more accessible evidence base – for example, through research synthesis – makes it more likely that the best evidence to date will be available when required. Nurturing the relationships between policy-makers and researchers increases their mutual trust, enabling researchers to drip-feed best evidence to date to policy-makers on the understanding that it is used cautiously and that the conclusions may change as more evidence emerges in future.

Effective dissemination and knowledge transfer activities demand further time from researchers that is only rarely reflected in research funding. The increasing emphasis on research impact has been operationalized through such programmes as TLRP, with its emphasis on impact and user engagement, and other initiatives outside education (see CHSRC n.d.; ESRC 2010b). Increasingly, funders are requiring grant applications to include plans for user engagement and impact. These developments are going some way towards improving the resourcing of dissemination and transfer activities.

Personal factors

Kirst (2000), drawing on a study of one education think tank located in a US university, noted that the effectiveness of external agents in providing information to appropriate users, and promoting its use, depends not so much on relative location (i.e. internal versus external), but on *who they are*, individually and institutionally. This was confirmed by a systematic review (Innvaer *et al.* 2002), which supports the notion that personal contact between researchers and decision-makers can be the most important facilitator of research in policy deliberations. Knott and Weissert (1996) identified the most critical determinants of an external agent's effectiveness as: being seen as credible colleagues who possess acknowledged expertise; familiarity with the users' institutional and practical problems; being in close enough proximity to be consulted when needed; and the type of organization from which they come – primarily research, policy or technical or some combination of these.

Tensions in engaging policy-makers

Engaging policy-makers in research is a major challenge partly because of practical issues relating to the limited time available to policy-makers, the location of the research and the research skills required. Policy-makers do not always know what is researchable. However, the challenge is exacerbated by low levels of trust, lack of awareness by some policy-makers of how different types of research knowledge may be used or simply because too little attention has been paid by researchers to understanding the interface. At the end of the seminars we concluded that there is a dearth of research on the social practices of decision-making in relation to the use of research in the policy community.

Is co-construction of knowledge between researchers and policy-makers feasible? If so, what is being co-constructed – the research evidence, dissemination, implementation or all of these? Can power relationships ever be equal in a funder–researcher relationship? A few recent publications from the Labour government's Department for Children, Schools and Families (DCSF) list staff alongside researchers as the authors. From the analysis of research in TLRP it emerged that the conceptual development that researchers might be trying to achieve can be in conflict with the expectations of the cooperating local authorities (local policy-makers). Policy-makers are potentially very powerful but operate, at times, with an agenda that has different and opposing objectives to those of the researchers. The seminars concluded that the distribution of power within the decision-making system is constantly changing and this needs to be acknowledged and taken into account by the research community.

One challenge identified here may be how to build relationships of mutual trust between policy and research communities so that tentative findings and conceptual framings may be brought into conversations between the two communities. As Winch (2001) noted, the public and political perception of education is that it is of practical relevance and will therefore be judged on its ability to say something relevant. Researchers have a moral obligation he claims, to ensure that they do not drop their standards of research to meet these requirements:

> [T]hey have a responsibility to do what they have been funded to do, to the best of their ability. This involves a responsibility to engage in reflection on these issues . . . without at the same time compromising their own values and beliefs. It is very often flattering to be asked to engage in this kind of high-level reflection by, for example, a government and there seem to be two temptations to avoid when doing so. The first is that of giving one's audience what one thinks it wants to hear, so as to maximise one's influence, prestige and the chances of being asked to engage in similar reflection in the future. Second, there is the opposite temptation of remaining 'excessively true to oneself' and failing to take a view of the matter which extends beyond one's own ideal of what should be the case.
>
> (Winch 2001: 449–50)

Rigby's (2005: 208) panellists from Capitol Hill identified similar issues:

> Most emphasised the importance of researchers 'staying clean' in order to maintain credibility, although one observed that while it is possible to keep research clean, it is impossible to keep a researcher clean, because of the value bias inherent in everyone.

The tension between presenting findings of the research to policy-makers but stopping short of drawing out direct policy implications on the basis that this is the role of the policy maker, has also been referred to by Kirst (2000: 386):

> While the social scientist's task is not to write policy, social
> science research intended for policymakers can identify and
> elaborate policy alternatives, stress their relative advan-
> tages, and point to positive courses of action or state context
> obstacles.

Some might suggest that this is a step too far for researchers
who lack the familiarity with the political, and sometimes economic, context needed to make a realistic assessment of the policy
alternatives.

Lessons learned and ways forward

Greater user engagement does not guarantee greater subsequent
use of research. More attention needs to be paid to working out the
conflicting interests of researchers and policy-makers, both during
the research and when there are outputs to share. User engagement
with policy-makers takes time to negotiate and sustain and, unless
expectations are managed, the policy-makers may orient the project
to meet their immediate needs rather than those reflected in the
longer-term aims of the research programme. Managing the tension
so that user engagement enhances the research programme seems
to demand a new set of skills for researchers.

In practical terms, the engagement of policy-makers in the
research process has been effective through involvement in generating and developing the research question, involvement in
research design (such as discussion of possible samples) and
research development, acting as a conduit between researchers and
services that are potential data sources (e.g. schools, districts, local
authorities, etc.) and verifying interpretations of emerging findings.
Each research project or programme needs to be explicit about the
purposes of the user engagement proposed at different stages of the
research process and about what is it trying to achieve.

Less frequently articulated is the contribution that policy-makers
can make to the longer-term development of a robust evidence base.
One conclusion emerging from the analyses of the TLRP programme
was the need for researchers to have an ongoing focus on the endur-
ing issues so as to generate resources that policy-makers can draw
on to deal with specific problems. The use of 'issue networks' (for
example, the TLRP science network [TLRP n.d.]) emerge from the
literature as effective. This resonates with Landry et al.'s (2003)

finding from a large survey of policy-makers, which concluded that it is consistent bodies of evidence being built up, rather than individual studies, that tend to be most influential in the development of policy. Furthermore, Knott and Weissert (1996) noted that single sources are demonstrably ineffective purveyors of social science knowledge to policy-makers. So, for example, reducing poverty, closing the attainment gap, effective methods of teaching reading or mathematics, and developing effective educational leaders are all areas in which many research teams are working. These are ongoing issues unlikely to disappear. Building the evidence base in these areas ensures that when a policy-maker needs the research, evidence can be made available in a timely manner.

This has implications for the undertaking of replication studies. Nutley, in her presentation to the seminar, distinguished between three different types of replication: *strict replication* – in which users are engaged in order to achieve commitment and ownership; *adapted replication* – which is of two types: either *what works principles*, interpreted by users in local contexts, or *scientific realist replication*, in which users are engaged to examine the interaction between context and programme mechanisms; finally, *relativist replication* – in which users are involved in negotiation of the meaning of a phenomenon and what counts as replication. It is much easier to obtain funding for new research than for any kind of replication and yet the need to strengthen the existing evidence base emerges throughout the literature. Greater collaborative working between research funders may assist in addressing this dilemma.

The role of systematic reviewing and involvement of policy-makers in some aspects of systematic reviewing (e.g. determining the question) can make an important contribution to strengthening the evidence base. Braye and Preston-Shoot (2005), who contributed to the seminar series, have developed an approach to systematic reviewing that includes non-research-based evidence in the form of the testimonies of 'experts by experience' (i.e. service users and carers), which was discussed in Chapter 4. They saw this as challenging the epistemological assumptions of systematic review methodology in various ways, in particular, in relation to the assumption of a hierarchy of evidence in which randomly controlled trials are always the gold standard.

Social networks emerge as critical to effective user engagement of policy-makers. These are multiple and include those between researchers and policy-makers, funders and researchers, funders and policy-makers, and policy organizations with each other. Finally, there is a growing group in education – longer established in political science – of intermediaries, also referred to as knowledge brokers (Cooper and Levin 2010), research mediators and third parties. In the policy context, these include individual 'experts', think tanks, commissions, political advisors, representatives from the media and what Brown (2009) refers to as 'insider-researchers' (researchers employed in government departments and agencies). These people have variable, but largely unknown and unaccountable, influence (Ball and Exley 2010) and, as in Kirst's think tank, may be an established group of researchers in one or more universities who also operate as a think tank. The relationships and networking that they manage to establish with both policy-makers and researchers can enhance or distract effective user engagement.

It was argued in the seminars that in a field like education, valuable knowledge often resides in the person (i.e. the researcher) rather than in a file or publication. Senior research analysts participating in the seminar series stressed the importance of trust in policy-makers' relationships with individual researchers. Kirst (2000) noted that experience in government made a noticeable difference to effectiveness, enabling the researchers to be credible, to empathize with policy officials, and to know when to intervene in the policy process. The advantages of secondments across and amongst different professional contexts within the research and policy landscape, though small in number to date, were highlighted as a means of developing this. The Commission on the Social Sciences (2003) recommended increasing the programme of secondments in both directions between staff in academia and those in government as a means of creating greater mutual understanding and knowledge transfer. It also recognized the increasing involvement of academics on research steering groups, advisory groups and other work in government.

Summary

This chapter has suggested who might be the policy users of research. It has presented models of research use in policy-making and summarized some of the empirical studies that inform our understanding of these. It has looked at the characteristics of research, researchers and policy-makers that inhibit or enhance research use and the role of user engagement in this. Finally, the tensions involved in engaging policy-makers in research and some lessons learned have been discussed to inform our thinking about constructive ways forward.

PART III
WHAT ARE THE IMPLICATIONS?

Chapter 6

Implications for researchers and research processes

This chapter looks at the implications of user engagement for members of the research community and for the practice of doing research. We outline ideas for change in four areas: research design and project management (greater recognition for the flow and interplay of different kinds of knowledge), researchers' skills and expertise (stronger emphasis on 'know who' and 'know when' as core research skills), research capacity building (clearer focus on user engagement in research training and project management), and research careers (support for user engagement activities and boundary crossing).

Research design and project management

Throughout this book we have sought to emphasize the idea that user engagement both demands and presents opportunities for new understandings of the research process. As such, user engagement has important implications for the ways in which research is designed and managed. Most importantly, user engagement requires much more careful thinking about how research design and project management can support the flow and interplay of different kinds of knowledge within and beyond research studies.

Knowledge processes as central to research design

If, as we have argued, knowledge exchange processes are at the heart of user engagement, then research design and planning needs to incorporate careful consideration of the dynamics of different kinds of knowledge within the research process. There are, however, different ways of thinking about the roles of research-based knowledge and other kinds of knowledge within research projects. One approach is to think of research and other kinds of educational work as different practices where care needs to be taken to manage knowledge across practice boundaries. As discussed in Chapter 3 with respect to practitioner engagement, this approach raises a number of questions that need considering as part of the research design process (Box 6.1). These concern the creation of fora for the exchange of different kinds of knowledge amongst different players within the process and the management of the interactions that take place within these fora at different stages during research projects.

Box 6.1   Knowledge flow issues for research design

- Why is two-way knowledge flow necessary for this study?
- When should knowledge move across research–practice and research–policy boundaries?
- Who will manage the interface where research and practice/policy meet?
- Who should meet at the interface?
- Do different groups need to meet at different times in the research process?
- How should research-based knowledge be represented at meetings?
- How can these meetings be used to further inform both research and practice/policy?

An alternative to this 'managing knowledge across boundaries' approach is to see the research process in terms of an ongoing process of knowledge co-construction within field-based educational practices. Here, researchers and users may have different roles based on their specific expertise, but they are in constant contact, working together towards a shared understanding of what is going on in practices. This then raises slightly different questions for research design (Box 6.2).

Box 6.2   Knowledge co-construction issues for research design

- Has everyone involved agreed on the overarching purpose of the study?

- Does everyone involved understand the demands of this kind of research partnership?
- Has the school, college or department signed up to ensuring that these demands can be accommodated?
- Are different roles and responsibilities clear and agreed upon?
- Have the boundaries of the work been made clear? That is, is this a research project with time limits and objectives to meet?
- Is the timetable for research activity and interim outputs clear?
- Have all aspects of writing up the findings been discussed?

The common idea underlying both sets of boxed questions is that strategic thinking about the interplay of different forms of knowledge and expertise is critical to research design and research planning. In earlier chapters, we saw how various research designs can be helpful for developing more diverse research teams and more interactive research processes. Collaborative research with practitioners and service users, for example, has provided examples of projects informed by approaches including:

- *Theories of Change* – an evaluation design that has knowledge sharing between researchers and stakeholders at its core and that can help promote collaboration and engagement with practitioners and service users (Connell and Kubish 1998; Sullivan *et al.* 2002).
- *Action research projects around a common theme* – a strategy for combining individual practitioner studies as part of a wider thematic research project in ways that connect and integrate developments in practice with the development of general principles (e.g. Sutherland *et al.* 2007).
- *Design experiments* – an approach to pedagogical research involving the iterative design and testing of teaching strategies by teams of researchers, practitioners and other specialists aiming to improve practice and generate knowledge (Cobb *et al.* 2003; van den Acker *et al.* 2006).
- *Developmental Work Research* – a research methodology that aims to provoke change in organizational work systems through providing participants with evidence about their everyday work practices and analytical resources to question those practices (Engeström 2007, 2008).

These examples are far from an exhaustive list. Instead, they are four illustrations of the way in which certain research designs can be helpful in approaching the process of engaging users because of the explicit emphasis they place on the interweaving of researchers' and practitioners' or service users' knowledge. The key to this inter-weaving, though, lies not in the designs themselves but in the particular ways in which they are shaped, facilitated and managed.

Project management

With more diverse research teams and more interactive ways of working, the demands on project leaders in terms of orchestrating roles, brokering knowledge and building shared understandings become much greater. Skilful project management is therefore central to effective user engagement. The examples of projects discussed in this book have highlighted the particular significance of managing relationships, knowledge processes and time and resources. The importance of managing relationships stems from the fact that researchers, practitioners and service users will all approach a research venture from different starting points and with different perspectives, motivations, concerns and goals. A key challenge for project leaders is therefore to help project participants to make explicit their own understandings and to appreciate those of others. The issue here is building a shared understanding of the overarching goals of the project in a way that helps different groups of participants to work together. This requires clear recognition for 'the relational dimensions of knowledge generation' and the importance of processes and qualities such as 'face to face contact', 'commitment to resolve conflicts as they arise', 'honesty and willingness to listen' and 'flexibility of all actors' (Lencucha *et al.* 2010: 68).

The need to manage knowledge processes is reflective of the way in which user engagement involves bringing together different forms of expertise and specialist knowledge. Project management thus becomes a complex task of negotiating and mediating relevant knowledge within and beyond the research project. This brings to the fore issues such as creating and managing fora for productive knowledge sharing amongst participants, understanding and coordinating the role of different kinds of expertise at different stages in the research process, and establishing and facilitating processes for the exchange and development of ideas with decision-makers and other users beyond the project team.

Finally, managing time and resources is critically important because of the time, energy and effort that is required by collaborative processes. Added to this is the need for ongoing negotiation of issues of timescale (e.g. predefined research schedules versus emerging lines of enquiry from project partners) and timing (e.g. the researcher's desire for conclusive findings versus the decision-maker's desire for timely advice).

The underlying point is that user engagement processes have important implications for the management of projects and the capabilities of project leaders. There are close parallels here with changing conceptions of project management practices more generally. Across the engineering and physical sciences, for example, instrumental images of 'projects as a linear sequence of tasks' are being superseded by ones focused much more on 'social interaction among people' (Winter *et al.* 2006: 644). With this comes greater recognition for the influence of 'social agendas, practices, stakeholder relations, politics and power' and the need for project leaders who can 'conceptualise projects from different perspectives, read situations, deal with ambiguity [and] relate to wider issues' (Winter *et al.* 2006: 642, 646).

Researcher skills and expertise

One of the key implications stemming from the discussions within this book is the need for a broader understanding of the skills and expertise that are required to be an effective researcher in education and other social sciences. We see the development of two forms of researcher expertise as particularly relevant for user engagement: 'know who' and 'know when'. These are both relational forms of expertise that, as argued earlier, need recognition as core research skills alongside the more established professional competences of 'know what', 'know why' and 'know how' (Lundvall 1996, 2000).

Know who

Throughout this book we have seen the influential role that the affective and the relational can play in user engagement. References to issues such as interpersonal interactions, values and trust, brokerage and mediation all underline the social nature of involving users in and with research. They also flag up the importance of what we and others have called 'know who' skills and expertise. Lundvall (1996: 8) characterizes 'know who' in terms of 'the social capacity to establish relationships to specialised groups in order to draw on their expertise'.

This kind of professional competence relates very closely to the demands of larger and more diverse research teams that are often associated with user engagement. The research process becomes one that involves and is shaped by a much wider range of players, each beginning from different starting points and having different motivations, perspectives, skill sets and knowledge. The challenges associated with developing and managing the roles and interactions between different players and forms of expertise are central to user engagement and the notion of 'know who'.

'Know who' also relates well to the significance of the personal in research utilization processes. We have seen in earlier chapters how practitioners' and policy makers' engagement with research is aided by 'interpersonal and social interactions' (Davies *et al.* 2008: 189) and 'sustained contacts based on personal relationships' (ESRC 2009a: 14). These underline the need for researchers to be skilled in nurturing productive professional relationships with research users and negotiating the kinds of dilemmas and tensions that can arise as part of these. We've heard, for example, how interacting with the policy process can challenge researchers in terms of 'compromising their own values and beliefs' (Winch 2001: 450) and how practitioners can feel 'a sense of isolation and faltering confidence' in engaging with research (Kahn *et al.* 2006: 9).

Another dimension of 'know who' is an appreciation of the diversity of research user communities and the nuances of different roles and positions within them. As noted in the opening chapter, user engagement needs to be informed by careful thinking about the very specific kinds of expertise (both professional and other) that might contribute to a particular research process. The key here is not just 'knowing who', but 'knowing how to know who' in very specific terms.

Know when

Another form of expertise and skill that is central to managing user engagement is the ability to negotiate issues of timescale, timing and time, what we have called 'know when'. As we have seen in earlier chapters, the contrasting timescales and rhythms of research, policy and practice can present real challenges for user engagement. While research projects usually have quite tightly planned schedules, engaging with the ideas and insights of users can open up new avenues or problems with trajectories and time-scales of their own. Being able to negotiate a path between the dynamics of emerging lines of enquiry and the requirements of original research objectives can be a crucial skill.

Another dimension of 'knowing when' concerns the timing or currency of research topics and ideas. During the seminar series, several of the policy-maker presenters underlined the importance of 'knowing when' in terms of spotting the emerging hot issues and topics, waiting for the moment when a senior policy person is looking for something that you can provide, and getting involved when ideas are in development or formation. Others talked about the knack of being in a place where others might enquire about what your research could do for them.

Finally, 'know when' is important in terms of the time that is required to negotiate and sustain engagement processes with practitioner and policy colleagues and other wider users. A number of the researchers who took part in the seminar series stressed how difficult it can be to find the time and space to do engagement, dissemination and knowledge transfer activities.

Core research skills

For both of the above forms of expertise, what became clear during the seminar series was that they are not necessarily areas of strength amongst social science researchers. For example, 'knowing how to know who' in order to take research findings and the ideas generated and refined in studies within reach of policy, was a source of considerable frustration across research projects discussed. This was echoed by other presentations from senior government or think tank representatives who described how national policy-makers rely primarily on commissions, trusted experts and think tanks, rather than academics, for ideas.

There is therefore a need, not only for increased awareness of 'know who' and 'know when', but also for these forms of relational expertise to be seen as *core research skills*. While there is greater awareness of what the ESRC refer to as 'skills for engaging with users and for maximizing the impact of research' (ESRC 2009c:

Annex 2), there is a danger of these capacities being seen as additional, rather than integral, to the core training of early career researchers. It's all too easy for example, for work on, 'research communication', 'working with the media' or 'getting research used' to be dealt with separately from issues such as 'research design', 'data collection' and 'data analysis'. So taking the latest ESRC guidance on social science research skills (Box 6.3), our argument is that development of the last three bullet points needs to be intricately connected with development of the first three. In other words, 'know who' and 'know when' need to be at the core of what it means to be a researcher and covered as part of the core business of research design, project management and methodological training.

Box 6.3 ESRC guidance on social science research skills

The overall goal of the training will be the development of fully trained and competent social science researchers, who have:

- a competent understanding of the debates within disciplines that inform their field of study
- a general overview of the philosophy of research methods and how this informs research design, the methods chosen, the means of analysis and the representation and presentation of information and data
- an ability to understand and use a range of research techniques appropriate to their subject area, and who are conversant and sympathetic to approaches used by other social scientists
- an ability to integrate what they have learned in addressing research in ways that are characteristic of an experienced highly effective researcher
- an appreciation of the potential use and impact of their research within and beyond academia
- an ability to engage with relevant users at all points in the research process, from devising and shaping research questions through to informing users' efforts to improve practice
- an ability to communicate their research findings effectively to a wide range of audiences.

Source: ESRC 2009c: 10–11

Research capacity building

The seminar series that led to this book helped to flag up a range of priorities for capacity building relating to user engagement. Clearly these will play out differently at different stages in researchers' careers. Three key areas, though, are the training of early career researchers, the development of project managers and the development of relational capacity *between* researchers and users.

Research training

We see a general need for the content of research training courses to have a better balance between knowledge generation and knowledge utilization. In other words, alongside developing expertise in the theory, methods and skills of doing research, early career researchers also need opportunities to develop knowledge, understanding and experience in user engagement and research mediation and use.

What might this mean for the average research training course? We see a number of ways in which existing knowledge generation issues could be extended to include knowledge mediation and use issues (Box 6.4). This rebalancing also needs to play out in the practical experiences that research students are required or encouraged to have during their courses. Priorities here might include:

- opportunities to develop and participate in user networks (subject associations, policy fora, media networks) as well as academic networks (conferences, seminars);
- encouragement to generate practical research outputs (briefings, toolkits, teaching resources, diagnostics) as well as academic research outputs (journal articles);
- the chance to work within teams of professionals in practice/policy organizations as well as within research groups in universities/research organizations.

Box 6.4   Covering user engagement issues in research training courses

- Learning about different forms of knowledge could be linked with learning about different models of research utilization.
- Discussions about appraising methodological validity could move on to discussions about assessing research use and impact.
- Developing skills in conducting interviews or surveys could sit alongside developing skills in creating research-informed resources for practice.
- Gaining experience of generating conclusions from research findings could be matched with gaining experience of working with stakeholders to formulate research questions.
- Thinking about research strategy in terms of a 'research questions and research methods' matrix could be extended to include thinking about research teams in terms of a 'research participants and forms of expertise' matrix.

All of these suggestions are about research training courses taking the knowledge, skills and understandings that are connected with user engagement more seriously. It is about providing opportunities for early career researchers to develop the subtle process skills associated with 'know who' and 'know when' as part of their core research training activities. There are strong connections here with the ESRC's calls for research training institutions to 'integrate transferable skills training into their doctoral programmes' and 'develop "people flow" initiatives for postgraduate students' (ESRC 2009c: 3). Likewise, the emphasis on 'greater flexibility in the timing of training delivery' (9) sits well with the gradual approach that is needed to developing and refining the sorts of skills and expertise that are associated with user engagement.

Project management

A recurring theme in this and earlier chapters has been the ways in which user engagement processes cast project management in a new light. When user engagement is understood as bringing together different types of expertise and specialist knowledge, then project management becomes a complex task of negotiating and mediating relevant knowledge both into and out of research projects. The skills and expertise associated with such brokerage therefore need explicit coverage within training opportunities for senior researchers. Changing the nature of postgraduate training courses is not enough on its own. As pointed out by the user members of the 2008 Research Assessment Exercise (RAE) Sub-Panel for Education, 'opportunities for research training for established staff' is just as important an indicator of capacity building within the field as provision for early career researchers (RAE 2008: 10).

There is a critical need, then, for project management training that gives serious attention to the skills and challenges that are associated with user engagement. Recent guidance on researcher career development cites 'the intellectual leadership of research projects' as a key responsibility of principal investigators (Concordat to Support the Career Development of Researchers 2008: 6). Our argument is that such intellectual leadership needs to relate as much to 'know who' and 'know when' (knowledge mediation and utilization) as it does to 'know what', 'know how' and 'know why' (knowledge generation). Courses in research project management and advanced research methodology therefore need to encompass and make explicit their coverage of issues such as:

- the significance of relational expertise ('know who' and 'know when') in leading research projects;
- the roles that different kinds of expertise can play at different stages in the research process and how their interplay can be coordinated;
- how users and researchers can be helped to identify and communicate the nature and limits of their expertise during a project;
- strategies for managing possible tensions between research objectives and emerging lines of enquiry or amongst the rhythms of research, policy and practice.

Project leaders also have an important responsibility for facilitating the learning of other members of project teams; the *Concordat to Support the Career Development of Researchers* (2008: 10) states that, 'research managers should actively encourage researchers to undertake Continuing Professional Development (CPD) activity, so far as is possible within the project'. In the context of user engagement, this is about recognizing opportunities for the development of new relational knowledge and expertise amongst project members and making effective use of people's existing strengths and talents in these areas. It is also about recognizing that 'educational researchers [and users] have diverse profiles in terms of age, experience and qualifications, and will be at different stages in their careers' (BERA 2008: 9).

As well as explicit training provision, there is also a need for more opportunities for informal exchange of expertise between experienced researchers. The Education RAE Sub-Panel reported 'a rich array of other research-focused services to support local, national and international education systems, working with policy-makers, practitioners, parents and students' (RAE 2008: 5). What is needed is more fora for the sharing of the process skills and expertise that are developing through such activities within and beyond the field of education. As a recent investigation into the humanities and social sciences concluded,

> [t]here is scope to develop initiatives to share examples of good practice across disciplines. [The research councils] should jointly convene workshops, bringing together researchers from across the humanities and social sciences disciplines to share their ideas and experiences for contributing to policy development.
>
> (British Academy 2008: xii)

Relational capacity

Finally, it is important to stress that the development of research capacity is not solely a process for researchers in isolation. A clear focus on enhancing the skills and understandings of early career and established researchers is critical, but so too are opportunities for shared training involving researchers *and* users. Within the educational research field there is clear recognition of the potential for 'regional collaboration on doctoral research training' (RAE 2008: 5; see also ESRC 2009c), but this could usefully be extended to training collaborations with user organizations (public services, government, business and third sector) as well as other universities. We realize that this is not an easy development to initiate, but it seems crucial that the trend towards research teams with more diverse researcher and user members needs to be matched by training courses with more diverse researcher and user participants.

Research careers

The final issue for consideration is the careers of researchers. This stems from the fact that user engagement raises questions about researcher identity (i.e. what it means to be an educational/social science researcher) and highlights the material conditions within which researchers operate. Put simply, it is clear that several aspects of researchers' current career structures are detrimental to the development of more and better user engagement within educational/social science research. We see an urgent need for improved recognition for user engagement-type activities and greater support for boundary crossing amongst the worlds of research, policy and practice as part of more varied research careers.

Recognition and incentives

In relation to recognition for user engagement-type activities, the British Academy's (2008) inquiry into practices across humanities and the social sciences stated clearly that

> [u]niversities should examine their criteria for academic promotion, with a view to including public policy engagement (and engagement with other research users) as a factor to be taken into account (as appropriate to the discipline).
>
> (xii)

It also argued that

> [h]igh-level recognition of contributions to better links between researchers and users could be helpful. Awards could raise the profile of the contributions that humanities and social science research can make to public policy development and the quality of life.
>
> (British Academy 2008: xv)

We see both of these measures – promotion criteria and incentives/ awards – as crucial for enhancing the profile and quality of user engagement in fields such as education.

Varied career routes

Any support for involvement in user engagement, however, needs to be part of a wider culture of encouragement for more varied researcher career routes that embrace 'new social identities [and] transcend fixed roles (such as "producers" and "users" of knowledge') (Saunders 2007b: xxi). What became clear during the seminar series that informed this book was that there is an increasing multiplicity of professional roles and identities that go beyond existing professional groupings. This reflects the fact that a whole range of new brokerage or mediation organizations have emerged in the 'no-person's land' between research and policy and practice. With this, the potential career pathways for researchers and other professionals in the knowledge economy have become more varied and more complex. Within the field of education, for example, the established pathways of either 'a traditional academic lectureship, an educational research career, or an educational career which draws on research experience (e.g. in schools, local authorities or national agencies)' (BERA 2008: 9) have become less clear-cut and more complicated over recent years. There is therefore a need for research development policies and structures that are grounded in 'a broad-minded approach to researcher careers' (Concordat Support the Career Development of Researchers 2008: 10) and recognize the benefits that can stem from working on the boundaries of different communities and career pathways.

Summary

This chapter has looked at what user engagement means for being a researcher and doing research. We have argued that user engagement both demands and presents opportunities for:

- more careful consideration of how research design and project management can support the interplay of different kinds of knowledge within the research process;
- greater recognition for the importance of 'know who' and 'know when' within researchers' skills and expertise ;
- better coverage of the skills and knowledge related to user engagement in training courses for early career researchers, project leaders and research users;
- improved recognition for user engagement-type activities within research career structures and more support for varied career routes and boundary crossing.

Chapter 7

Implications for users of research

This chapter highlights the implications of our discussion for each of the main user groups that we have identified – practitioners, service users and policy-makers (including funders). We look in particular at initiatives that build on existing social networks, which have emerged as a critical factor in establishing and sustaining user engagement. Four major implications are presented: the need for better intelligence about users, clearer expectations of users to engage in research, stronger capacity amongst users to do so, and improved infrastructure to support such processes. The chapter concludes that engagement in research is supported by an organizational infrastructure that is research minded and that can improve both the use of research and the quality of the services that this research informs.

It is all too easy to focus on the implications for research and researchers while overlooking messages for users, their institutions and, where relevant, their professions. In Chapter 1, we provided the definition of 'user' that we have adopted through the rest of the book. We acknowledged the use of broad categories such as 'policy-makers', within which there is a range of users such as politicians, senior officials, funders and within-government researchers, each having very different interests. Hence, it is important to emphasize the heterogeneity within each category of user. In this chapter, some implications for all these groups are considered.

We see four major implications for research users. These highlight the need to develop:

- better *intelligence* about users and engagement strategies
- clearer *expectations* of users to engage in and with research
- stronger *capacity* amongst users for research engagement
- improved *infrastructure* and support for user engagement.

Intelligence about users and engagement strategies

To increase user engagement with and in research, practitioners and service users need to take greater control of the research agenda and make demands on both funders (who are themselves users) and researchers to recognize their needs in formulating research questions. This will provide intelligence about both the needs of users and the strategies for engagement that might be effective. In Chapter 2, we noted that we know little about some of the epistemic cultures that comprise education as it is practised, which are diverse and need to be understood and incorporated into the processes of knowledge co-construction. This, we suggest, facilitates mutual learning across research–practice boundaries. We have not suggested that *all* users can be meaningfully engaged in research: rather, that extending user engagement has the capacity to improve the quality of research and that of education as well as increasing the use made of the findings from research.

Hence, the potential users for each specific study or body of research should express their needs explicitly in order for researchers to consider how they might be involved more effectively. For example, older people, who were the focus of Barnes and Taylor's (2007) research reviewed in Chapter 4, merit a different approach to the teachers or social workers considered in Chapter 3. Within each of these groups there will be a range of motivations to become involved in research, and a variety of previous knowledge and skills about research and potential implications for the individual, profession or service arising from the research. In Chapter 2, we suggested that questions be asked about what each group of users might want to know, how they might act on the knowledge that emerges and what role they might wish to take in the wider sharing of the findings.

With respect to intelligence about engagement strategies, it is helpful to distinguish between engaging *with* research and engaging *in* research across the approaches we have reviewed in previous chapters. In Chapter 3, we noted the importance of practitioners increasing their capacity to engage *with* research by developing their skills in critical inquiry. This will better prepare them for identifying relevant research and judging its quality. However, as we noted previously, to move from the individual practitioner activity of critically selecting existing research, to applying it in the process of scrutinizing practice, the organization will need to be research minded, otherwise the influence of the research is likely to remain minimal.

With respect to users engaging *in* research, the Theories of Change approach described in Chapter 3, initially adopted in evaluating community initiatives, is pertinent. In this approach to evaluation, knowledge-sharing is at the core. Potential research users are engaged by the researchers in discussion of what the initiative is intended to achieve. The relationship between researcher and user is prioritized to generate the research design and maximize validity through the use of 'local' experience. The implications of this are far-reaching and include:

- policy-makers bringing together service users and researchers prior to confirming the research focus;
- funders considering, as a few do currently, how knowledge-sharing could be used in the commissioning process to improve the quality and relevance of the research;
- users challenging researchers when approached and invited to participate in research, in order to clarify how their knowledge and experience can be taken into account in the design and thereafter in the data collection, analysis and interpretation.

Expectations of users to engage in and with research

The expectations of users to engage with and in research vary greatly for different users. This section considers in turn some different groups of users: funders, policy-makers, practitioners and service users.

Funders are expected to know about the current evidence base before commissioning further research but have very different approaches to supporting the use of the research that they fund. As Tetroe *et al.* (2008) have reported, only 30 per cent of the funders in their international survey, had strategies for evaluating the impact of the research that they commission.

Some policy-makers, as we noted in Chapter 5, espouse the rhetoric of evidence-informed policy, but there is little riposte for either researchers or service users when policies are announced and rolled out that appear to lack any supporting evidence base. As previously noted, while the expectation of policy-makers to consider research might be seen as a moral obligation, the reality has to be assessed in a context in which many other factors – political, economic, media, public opinion, issues of timescale and of potential for scaling up – influence their behaviour. Some initiatives for increasing policy-makers' awareness and understanding of research, such as the National School of Government (http://www.nationalschool.gov.uk) Analysis and Use of Evidence programme for senior civil servants, are explored below in the section on capacity building.

Practitioners in education have no legal obligation to use research, although there are occasional examples of adults taking legal action against individual schools or local authorities retrospectively, for not using 'best evidence' to provide diagnosis and support for conditions such as autism or dyslexia. For example:

> [T]he failure of schools to diagnose and provide remedial help for dyslexia became grounds for personal injury litigation in 1999 following a House of Lords decision in the case of Pamela Phelps.
>
> (Anxiety Zone 2009)

In some professions such as medicine, there is a legal obligation to make use of research. The Royal College of General Practitioners' (RCGP 2006: 5) *Curriculum Statement 3.6* on research states:

> All GPs will be initiators, collaborators or users of research. In this context, the minimum competence required is that of a user. The effective user of research will be able to demonstrate competence in the following areas:
>
> • Prioritising relevant information
> • Critical appraisal
> • Problem framing
> • Accessing evidence
> • Implementing change in clinical practice.

It goes on to suggest that

> [a]ll GPs should be familiar with essential components of the research process. They should be able to:
>
> • Develop a research question
> • Identify appropriate methods from a range of designs

- Draw up a questionnaire
- Demonstrate basic quantitative and qualitative data analysis skills
- Draw appropriate conclusions
- Summarise results.

(6)

Furthermore, should a GP feel the need to update their research skills, they can enrol in the Research Capacity Development Programme, a national programme that provides personal training awards and funds academic infrastructure to support research capacity development within the National Health Service (NHS), funded by the Department of Health.

In contrast to this, the teaching standards in England (TDA 2007) for qualified teacher status make no reference to the use of research or evidence. The core standards for teachers who have completed their induction include knowing 'how to use local and national statistical information to evaluate the effectiveness of their teaching' (TDA 2007: 16).

Only for Excellent Teachers (a status ascribed to a small percentage of teachers who are recognized as a resource for other teachers, requiring experience, pedagogic excellence and coaching and mentoring skills), do the standards mention research. Standard E2 stipulates that Excellent Teachers can '[r]esearch and evaluate innovative curricular practices and draw on research outcomes and other sources of external evidence to inform their own practice and that of colleagues' (TDA 2007: 27). While the recently introduced Masters in Teaching and Learning offers some teachers potential for classroom-based research, previous schemes such as the Best Practice Research Scholarships, application to which was open to many teachers, are no longer available despite positive evaluations of its outcomes (Furlong and Salisbury 2005).

Hence, despite the Training and Development Agency for Schools' (TDA) previous slogan of 'an evidence-informed profession' and a previous government claiming a commitment to evidence-informed policy and practice, the teaching profession is not expected to use research, let alone given the resources or support to engage in it as a matter of course.

Service users are in general not expected to either use or engage in research. The possible exception is students at school, further or higher education who are expected to develop research skills as part of their learning. For service users in other contexts, a greater priority is to exercise their rights to influence research. Service users' experience of research is often limited to that reported by the more accessible media (e.g. broadsheets, television) and they are most likely to become more aware of it when the research focuses on their particular services, in which errors and misconceptions are more likely to be identified.

As Barnes and Taylor (2007) have noted, the right to be listened to provides the foundations for enabling service users to become engaged with research, in particular with articulating the issues that they believe should be the focus of research in their services. This right to be listened to has, for service users, become embedded in legislation and occupational standards in both children's and adult's services in the UK. For example, the National Occupational Standards in Children's Care, Learning and Development states that staff should '[L]isten to children and respond to them in a way that shows that you value what they say and feel' (CWDC 2004: 6).

Practitioners and service users, then, need to assert their perspectives in the research process such that others' expectation of them will be that they have a key contribution to make to research. In Chapter 3, we set out some questions that researchers should ask themselves when attempting to engage practitioners in co-construction of knowledge within field-based educational practices. Some of the same questions can be used by practitioners, policymakers and service users to explore researchers' expectations of the users' role in the research:

- Has everyone involved agreed on the overarching purpose of the study?
- Does everyone involved understand the demands of the research partnership?
- Has the service signed up to ensuring that these demands can be accommodated?
- Have the boundaries between the research and the service been made clear (e.g. that this is a service in which users have rights and responsibilities)?
- Is the timetable for research activity and interim outputs clear?
- Have all aspects of reporting, sharing and using the findings been agreed?

Users' capacity for research engagement

We noted in Chapters 3, 4 and 5 that a key issue in developing user engagement in research is the limitations in the capacity of users to engage with and, particularly, in research. What we mean by 'capacity' in this context is the skills, understanding and the resources available to users, such as time and access, which all affect their engagement with and in research. The capacity of different user groups – policy-makers, practitioners and service users are considered in turn.

There have been a number of initiatives for building capacity amongst policy-makers to use and engage in research. These include formal training opportunities for policy makers in the use of evidence. For example, the National School of Government (http://www.nationalschool.gov.uk) runs a programme for senior civil servants on analysis and use of evidence. The Institute of Education, University of London, runs a masters of science in policy analysis and evaluation (http://www.ioe.ac.uk/study/researchDegrees/RMS9_PAE999.html), which aims to provide a broad-based training in social science and recruits some policy-makers. In Ontario, The Evaluation and Research Learning Program (Ontario Ministry of Education 2010) consists of six modules that equip ministry staff and managers with the knowledge and ability to use research and evaluation effectively for decision-making. The participants are policy and programme staff. It is difficult to evaluate the effects of such programmes as information about the participants, completions and outcomes is not in the public domain. Other ways of building capacity have included secondments of researchers into government, of policy-makers out of government into research and of government insider researchers who are often analysts, to research teams that are based outside government.

For practitioners, there have been many initiatives, some reviewed in Chapter 3, for increasing their capacity to engage with and in research. Different models were reviewed in that chapter and the importance of sustained engagement was noted. McLaughlin *et al.* (2005), in their evaluation of networked learning communities, noted that practitioners' engagement *in* research does not necessarily lead seamlessly into practitioners' engagement *with* research. However, they noted that effective external support was used to access the knowledge base and that '[t]hose who engage in research and enquiry are more likely to use, and feel positive about using, others' research and enquiry findings' (4). They went on to conclude that the greater the significance of the impact of the research on an individual, classroom or school, the more likely it was to become embedded and to sustain further research. The key factors in building research capacity in practitioner communities were external support and facilitation, alignment of issues with the school and/or network learning community and effective leadership.

The involvement of teachers in both the TLRP and AERS programmes provided models for increasing the capacity for practitioners in these programmes – usually teachers – to engage in research. However, Taylor *et al.* (2007) noted in the interim evaluation of AERS that no budget existed for engaging teachers in the research networks and this limited the levels of engagement that could be established.

As Mitchell *et al.* (2010) noted in their useful systematic review of practitioner research studies in social work, the first challenge is identifying studies undertaken by individual, isolated practitioners who are less likely to publish the findings in academic or even professional journals. For these practitioners, the evidence we have presented in this book suggests capacity building in research will involve building on existing networks (which may not initially have a research focus) to link them into an infrastructure that will support their activities. Through these networks, they might have opportunities to meet researchers, and share research priorities and training with them. This process will need, as noted in Chapter 3, to legitimize the questioning of practices and, indeed, build such questioning into the practices themselves. This is key to changing the practices and encouraging the generation of new knowledge.

For service users, as with the engagement of the general public with research, a critical issue is the understanding of types of evidence and research. There is widespread confusion about the differences amongst types of evidence, what they can tell us, their limitations and potential use. This is eloquently illustrated in the statement from the House of Commons proceedings (Goldacre 2009: 16) from the (then) Liberal Democrat MP Evan Harris (a doctor), who introduced evidence into the parliamentary debate on cancer screening by saying 'The honourable member for Braintree cited evidence from the *Sun*, so I want to refer to a recent edition of the *British Medical Journal*.' Developing better public understanding of the nature of evidence is critical in our development as a democratic society. Policy-makers, practitioners and service users are making decisions on a daily basis with poor capacity to distinguish commentaries, inspection evidence, single studies, reviews or meta-analysis. The organization Sense about Science (http://www.senseaboutscience.org.uk/index.php) is a charitable foundation that addresses misrepresentation of that science and scientific evidence which is regarded as important to society. More such initiatives would seem necessary if this major capacity problem is to be addressed.

For most general public users of research, the representation of evidence in the media may be their only source of information. Hence, Levin (2004b), in his analysis of the relationships amongst research, government and the media, notes that the media has a tendency to simplify findings, assign blame, and be focused mainly on the short term. Levin's research programme at the University of Toronto, Ontario Institute for Studies in Education, Research Supporting Practice in Education (http://www.oise.utoronto.ca/rspe/index.html), has set up Facts in Education, a service that aims to correct significant factual errors about education that appear in news media sources across Canada and to increase awareness of the correct information. A panel of experts use well-established bodies of information to address the issues and provide further reading. A posting on their blog on 1 April 2010 provides an interesting example:

The Facts on School Choice and Decentralization
Why school boards should follow Edmonton's lead: Allowing parents more choice is a welcome change from the 'one size fits all' model imposed on neighbourhoods by public school boards. Published in the Globe and Mail.

(Facts in Education 2010)

Facts in Education provided this response:

This article makes the claim that, 'If Toronto and other urban school boards follow Edmonton's lead, Canadians could see a revolution take place in the quality of education provided to our children.' Although there are many reasons to support, or not support decentralization and school choice in Canada, the body of evidence does not support the view that either decentralization or school choice alone will produce significant improvements in student outcomes.

This is followed by the signatures of the panellists and references to the evidence. It is too early to assess this interesting initiative, but it appears to be an encouraging example that might be built upon.

Infrastructure and support for research engagement

In Chapter 2, we described the creation of sustained fora where researchers and policy specialists could meet, and where both 'know who' and common knowledge could be built.

In Chapter 3, we noted the need to shift the emphasis to how both research and practice can be mutually informed during a research study, in which working closely with the field of practice can strengthen educational research as it allows researchers to keep in touch with current intentions in practices. Educational practitioners engaging in research alongside university-based researchers can help create their capacity for purposeful questioning of practices and contribute to innovation. However, much of this activity is short-lived and hard to sustain due to the resources required. Hence, infrastructures that support research–user interfaces are critical in facilitating greater and more sustainable user engagement. These infrastructures are now examined in relation to funders, practitioners and service users in turn.

Funders are both commissioners and users of research. They may also act as intermediaries through their relationship with the press, contact with government and promotion of networks. Tetroe *et al.* (2008), in the context of health care, suggests involving end users in prioritizing research topics for commissioned research. Some Canadian national granting agencies have followed this lead by requiring active decision-maker participation on grant submissions (see, for example, the Canadian Institutes of Health Research's *Knowledge Translation Strategy 2004–2009* www.cihr-irsc.gc.ca/e/26574.html). Similarly, in England, for example, the Nuffield Foundation (www.nuffieldfoundation.org), a key funding charitable foundation in the social sciences, is very active in dissemination activities but also uses its vast networks to set up seminars prior to the finalizing of research reports. These seminars seek to verify interpretations of the findings from a wide range of users and other researchers, prior to publication. The diverse culture of research commissioners makes understanding funders' perceptions of research needs, a major challenge for researchers.

The OECD/CERI (2002) report referred to funders' research needs in England as 'use-inspired'.

Funders are increasingly demanding plans for user engagement within applications for research grants. For example, the Nuffield Foundation, *Guide to Grants for Research and Innovation* includes the following:

> Projects usually have more impact when those who are likely to be interested in the results are engaged at the early stages, ideally with the planning of the project. So *when you apply* we will look for evidence that you have identified those to whom the outcomes of the project will be most relevant, and have thought about how you will engage them.
>
> (Nuffield Foundation 2010: 17)

The ESRC requirements to applicants include asking them to:

> [d]etail how the proposed research project will be managed to engage users and beneficiaries and increase the likelihood of impacts. When completing the attachment, please consider and address the following if appropriate to research of this nature . . .

- How have beneficiaries been engaged to date, and how will they be engaged moving forward?
- How will the work build on existing or create new links?
- Outline plans to work with intermediary organisations or networks.

> What activities will be undertaken to ensure good engagement and communication? For example:

- Secondments of research or user community staff;
- Events aimed at a target audience;
- Workshops to provide training or information dissemination; and
- Publications and publicity materials summarising main outcomes in a way that beneficiaries will be able to understand and use;
- Websites and interactive media;

- Media relations;
- Public affairs activities.

(ESRC 2010a)

In addition, the ESRC now have a knowledge transfer team who commissions knowledge transfer activities. Similar developments have taken place amongst funding agencies in parts of North America and, in particular, Canada. What is less clear is how far these requirements are understood, both by researchers completing the applications and by those academic and user referees reviewing and assessing them.

Turning to infrastructures designed to support practitioners' engagement in research, the National Teacher Research panel, set up in 1999 and consisting of practising teachers and head teachers with research expertise who work to promote teacher involvement in research, support quality in practice-based research and encourage partnership between teachers and researchers in England. They run major national conferences at which teacher research is presented, provide user perspectives on research proposals and draft reports for funders, and challenge policy-makers and researchers in the process of identifying research priorities.

Another example of developing infrastructure to support user engagement with research is Journal Watch (see Gough *et al.* 2009). A group of researchers and practitioners in child welfare search journals monthly and review them during videoconferences. They then prepare short reviews of exceptional articles that are shared, in an electronic newsletter, with the broader community of child welfare researchers and practitioners across Canada. This group is essentially mediating research for a wider audience and potentially training both new researchers and practitioners in critical inquiry.

The Researchers in Residence scheme (www.researchersin residence.ac.uk/cms) brings researchers and schools together to introduce school students to cutting-edge research in a particular field (e.g. climate change, genome research). Teachers and school students are introduced to the roles and skills of researchers who themselves develop the communication and presentational skills needed to disseminate their research to a wider audience beyond the academic community. Funded by Research Councils UK and the Wellcome Trust since 2005, researchers undertake placements in schools to benefit both the researcher and the school.

A different type of researcher in residence scheme involves researchers undertaking a regular or block placement in a school or with a group of schools, specifically to support teachers and other staff in using research and in undertaking small scale studies. For example, the Canadian Council on Learning and the Vancouver School Board launched a three-year partnership in 2007 to sponsor a researcher in residence to work with the district's Community and Inner City Schools projects (http://www.ccl-cca.ca/CCL/Research/ ResearcherinResidence). The research focused on supporting and tracking students at risk. The scheme is aimed explicitly at increasing the school board's research capacity at both the staff and district programme level. Both these models of researchers in residence provide an infrastructure to develop and support user engagement in research and in both cases the schools themselves are developing ways in which it can sustain support for research in the longer term.

As part of the knowledge management programme at the University of Toronto, Cooper and Levin (2010) noted that active efforts to facilitate learning about knowledge management include the building of collaborative interactions between researchers and practitioners in different disciplines and countries and the maintenance of a listserv for sharing ideas and resources (involving some one hundred people in ten countries). These authors suggest, however, that while networks are recognized as an effective medium through which to share knowledge and effect change, they are difficult to build and maintain. For instance, they note that participation and interaction in, and on, the University of Toronto's knowledge management listserv remains low. They also contend that while network participants, or potential participants, may express an interest in activities, in some cases they simply cannot find the time to participate to any significant degree. Thus they conclude that networks take resource and effort to nurture and maintain and that those interested in creating networks must take active steps to foster and facilitate involvement.

Phipps and Shapson (2009) reported that almost all academic institutions in Canada still lack the capacity to support research use in order to inform decisions about public policy and professional practice. Cooper and Levin (2010) similarly reported on the lack of infrastructure in institutions of higher education that support knowledge transfer, knowledge exchange and research use.

Infrastructure that supports service users' engagement in research includes ResearchImpact, a Canadian programme run by several universities, including York University and the University of Victoria in Toronto (www.researchimpact.ca/home/), a Canadian website run by the Knowledge Mobilization Unit at York University and the University of Victoria in Toronto that connects university researchers with policy-makers and community organizations who want to use research in the social sciences and humanities to inform their decision-making. Phipps and Shapson (2009) describe the work of this unit as involving two-way transformation, two-way engagement and the development of institutional capacity to support research-based social innovation and knowledge mobilization. One example reported on the ResearchImpact website is the Aboriginal Policy Research Forum, which took place on 14 January 2008 (see ResearchImpact 2008). The forum used broadband technology to bring together researchers, policy-makers and citizens from across the country to discuss Aboriginal issues. A key focus of the forum was the sharing of knowledge between diverse audiences, from academics to community decision-makers, which enabled the research to be informed by Aboriginal community priorities. In the area of environmental research, local Aboriginal communities have been engaged in helping researchers determine priorities that led to them securing food sources and improved well-being. Hence, for relatively little, if any, additional investment (since broadband is available in many areas), fora could be cultivated that enable meaningful co-research for conceptual development, of the type outlined in Chapter 2.

In Chapter 3 we set out three different models of research use from Walter *et al.* (2004). One of these, organizational excellence, describes institutions that support research use by developing an organizational culture that is 'research minded'. This can apply to organizations in which policy-makers, practitioners and service users work and, in some cases, live. In these institutions there is local adaptation of research findings and ongoing learning within the organization. Partnerships with local universities and intermediary organizations are used to facilitate both the creation and use of research knowledge. We previously referred to work by Nutley *et al.* (2007) suggesting that insufficient attention had been paid to organizational excellence in educational research. As Sharon Friesen, Galileo Educational Network (cited in Cabinet Office Strategy Unit 2009: 64) noted: '[w]here professionals are encouraged to lead and share innovation and research, the results are impressive – all those in the system start to invest in service improvement.' So, organizational excellence seems to provide a context in which infrastructure to support user engagement can develop and enable each of our groups of users to make a more meaningful contribution to the research process.

Summary

In this chapter we have drawn out the implications of previous chapters for users of research. In particular, we have considered the intelligence, expectations, capacity and infrastructure that support and enable potential users of research to engage with and in research. Each of these has been illustrated with recent developments that attempt to strengthen user engagement. We have noted that effective engagement may require users to take greater control of the research agenda and make demands on funders and researchers to recognize their needs throughout the research process. Finally, we conclude that establishing an infrastructure that develops an organizational culture that is research minded facilitates more extensive and meaningful user engagement.

Chapter 8

Concluding note

Having outlined the implications arising from this book for research-ers and research users, we now return to the four challenges for user engagement highlighted in the opening chapter. We use these challenges to consider briefly what we have learned about conceptualizing, managing, scaling up and evidencing user engagement.

Conceptualizing user engagement

We are in no doubt that the conceptualization of user engagement matters. Simplistic, understandings of 'users', 'engagement' or 'research', 'practice' and 'policy' are a poor basis from which to develop appropriate and effective approaches to engaging users in and with research. Throughout this book we have seen examples of the way in which the *how* (strategies, approaches) of user engagement needs to be informed by careful thinking about issues of *why* (the purposes and motives for different groups), *who* (nature and dynamics of different user groups), *what* (roles and contributions of different players) and *when* (sequencing of different contributions). Our view is that, in the contexts of social science and educational research, user engagement is helpfully conceived of as an interplay between the different kinds of knowledge and expertise held by researchers and different types of users. This is about thinking of research teams in terms of varied players, and research processes in terms of facilitating productive interactions amongst different kinds of knowledge, experience and expertise.

Taking such a perspective helps to strengthen the conceptual basis for discussing and developing user engagement in a number of ways. First, it places user engagement within the context of the need for research to be 'forward-looking' and 'speculative' as well as 'backward-looking' and 'evaluative' (Somekh 2007: 49). This helps to provide something of a trajectory for work in this area based on the idea of 'playing a different kind of game' (49). Second, it connects the development of user engagement with the development of research designs, which opens up a wide range of new conceptual and methodological resources. The concepts, tools, methods and theory associated with developments such as design experiments, Developmental Work Research, user-led research and Theories of Change evaluation are some of the examples given in this book. Third, it brings ideas relating to inter-professional and multidisciplinary working and knowledge exchange and co-construction into the realm of user engagement theory and practice.

None of the above purports that the challenge of becoming clearer about user engagement as a concept and a process is going to be easy. What this book is offering, though, is a richer toolbox of conceptual ideas and theoretical resources with which to approach and reflect upon collaborative work with users.

Managing user engagement

If user engagement is about bringing together different knowledge from a range of practices, then project management becomes the orchestration of this 'bringing together'. Skilled project management is therefore central to the development of effective user engagement. As pointed out in several of the previous chapters, this brings very real demands for project leaders in terms of managing relationships, managing knowledge processes and managing time and resources. In connection with such demands, this book has generated a number of starting points for future progress.

It has highlighted the significance of relational expertise in user engagement and begun to articulate what this means for project leadership. The key argument here is that intellectual leadership of research needs to relate as much to 'know who' and 'know when' (knowledge mediation/utilization) as it does to 'know what', 'know how' and 'know why' (knowledge generation). Following on from this, we have also flagged up the need for stronger recognition and support for user engagement in advanced project leadership. The kinds of priorities for attention and action that stem from this are:

- more explicit coverage of relational expertise ('know who' and 'know when') in training opportunities for senior researchers;

- more opportunities for the informal exchange of such experience and expertise amongst project leaders;
- clearer recognition from research funders and commissioners for the time and cost demands associated with effective user engagement.

Scaling up user engagement

At various points in this book we have touched on issues of scale, highlighting the ways in which user engagement can be limited by approaches that are superficial or very small in scale. In connection with the challenge of scaling up user engagement, we see two main learning points emerging from our discussion.

The first point is that any efforts to increase the scale of user engagement must not overlook steps to increase its depth or quality. This is about establishing strong foundations for scaling up through steps such as building user engagement and knowledge exchange into the core of research design and research methodology; seeing all aspects of the research process as potential fora for user engagement; fostering early and ongoing communication about different team members' motivations, interests, needs and concerns; and developing ethical and reflexive approaches to negotiating issues of power, roles and ownership during projects.

The second point concerns scaling up directly and is about enhancing the breadth or reach of user engagement. There are several issues in need of attention here. There is certainly a need for a stronger institutional dimension to user engagement concepts and practices. Finding ways of enabling knowledge co-construction by individual users and researchers to develop into similar knowledge exchange processes within and amongst institutions would be one example. There is also a need to improve the infrastructure surrounding user engagement initiatives. This is about taking seriously the ways in which users' and researchers' career structures, training provision, institutional incentives and professional standards could better support research collaboration and engagement. User engagement with research needs to be developed within the infrastructure of government, public and other services. For example, the expectation to use research needs to be built into the decision-making processes of government departments, school governing bodies, local authority committees and board meetings of charitable foundations. It also needs to be built into the professional standards and expectations throughout the professions, beyond medicine. Only through these embedded expectations can scaling up of user engagement in research become established at the systemic level.

Evidencing user engagement

We noted at the outset that user engagement is not particularly well evidenced in terms of empirical investigation or theoretical exploration. Throughout this book, we have therefore brought together various sources of information that help to illuminate different aspects of the processes and challenges of working with research users. We have drawn on evaluations of research programmes featuring user involvement (e.g. Taylor *et al.* 2007), reflexive accounts of various kinds of collaborations with practitioners (e.g. Kahn *et al.* 2006), service users (e.g. Braye and Preston-Shoot 2005) and decision-makers (e.g. Somekh 2007), empirical studies of related processes such as research impact (e.g. Cooper and Levin 2010) and knowledge mobilization (e.g. Phipps and Shapson 2009), and literature or knowledge reviews on evidence use (e.g. Nutley *et al.* 2007).

Taken together, however, these various sources do not represent a well-developed evidence base on the topic of user engagement. As Nutley *et al.* (2007: 316) put it, 'there is much yet to uncover [. . .] and further research has the potential to augment our understanding of [user engagement] processes, as well as to provide a richer, more nuanced evidence base on which to develop [user engagement] strategies'. In view of this, we see a clear need for user engagement initiatives to be evaluated and researched in their own right, especially ones involving different kinds of service users; more encouragement for reflexive accounts of user engagement processes, particularly covering their internal workings and relational dimensions; and more commitment to building and broadening the existing knowledge base about different kinds of user groups and different types of engagement strategies.

Appendix

Background on Thematic Seminar Series

The ideas in this book grew out of a thematic seminar series, 'Making a Difference: Working with Users to Develop Educational Research', that formed part of the UK Teaching and Learning Research Programme (TLRP). The series explored the implications of different forms of user engagement for the design of educational research. It aimed to develop the capacity of educational research to make a difference to policy and practice through better understanding and promotion of user involvement.

The series comprised five one-day seminars in 2005 and 2006 (see table below) that examined the TLRP experience (Seminar 1), the research–policy/funding interface (Seminar 2), the research–practice interface (Seminar 3), the wider social science context (Seminar 4) and the series' overall conclusions and implications (Seminar 5). The five seminars featured inputs from academics, practitioners, policy-makers and those involved in the mediation of research evidence.

Seminar	Title	Date/location
1	'Identifying Lessons for Research Design from Experiences of User Engagement in TLRP Projects and Scoping the Challenges for the Seminar Series'	2 March 2005 University of London, Institute of Education
2	'Knowledge Generation, Knowledge Management and the Links between Research and Policy'	24 May 2005 University of London, Institute of Education

(continued)

Seminar	Title	Date/location
3	'Research and Practitioners: People, Organisations and Systems'	10 October 2005 University of Birmingham
4	'What Can Education Learn about User Engagement from the Wider Social Science Community?'	8 March 2006 University of Oxford
5	'A Review of the Learning from the Previous Seminars with a Focus on the Implications for the Development of Educational Research'	15 June 2006 University of London, Institute of Education

Thematic summaries of each of the seminars as well as other documentation are available from the project website (www.tlrp. org/themes/seminar/edwards). Other published outputs include a research briefing (Edwards *et al.* 2009b), a book chapter (Sebba 2007) and journal articles (Edwards *et al.* 2006b, 2007).

Bibliography

Abelson, D. (2007) 'Any ideas? Think tanks and policy analysis in Canada', in L. Dobuzinskis, M. Howlett and D. Laycock (eds) *Policy Analysis in Canada: the state of the art*, Toronto: University of Toronto Press.

Ainscow, M., Booth, T., Dyson, A., Farrell, P., Frankham, J., Gallannaugh, F., Howes, A. and Smith, R. (2006) *Improving Schools, Developing Inclusion*, Abingdon: Routledge.

Amara, N., Ouimet, M. and Landry, R. (2004) 'New evidence on instrumental, conceptual, and symbolic utilization of university research in government agencies', *Science Communication,* 26(1): 75–106.

Anxiety Zone (2009) 'Dyslexia', *AnxietyZone*. Online. Available: http://www.anxietyzone.com/conditions/dyslexia.html (accessed 5 June 2010).

Ball, S. and Exley, S. (2010) 'Making policy with "good ideas": policy networks and the "intellectuals" of New Labour', *Journal of Education Policy,* 25(2): 151–69.

Barab, S. and Squire, K. (2004) 'Design-based research: putting a stake in the ground', *Journal of the Learning Sciences,* 13(1): 1–14.

Barnes, M. (2006) 'Researching with service users: a perspective from health and social policy', paper presented at Seminar 4 of the User Engagement Thematic Seminar Series, Maison Française d'Oxford, 8 March 2006.

Barnes, M. (2008) 'Is the personal no longer political? A response to Charles Leadbeater, Jamie Bartlett and Niamh Gallagher's "Making it Personal" (Demos, 2008)', *Soundings,* 39: 152–9.

Barnes, M. and Taylor, S. (2007) *Involving Older People in Research: examples, purposes and good practice*. Online. Available: http://www.era-age.group.shef.ac.uk/download.php?id=406 (accessed 23 March 2010).

Barnett-Page, E. and Thomas, J. (2009) 'Methods for the synthesis of qualitative research: a critical review', *BMC Medical Research Methodology* 9: 59.

Bartlett, J. (2009) 'At your service: navigating the future market in health and social care'. Online. Available: http://www.demos.co.uk/files/At_your_service_-_web.pdf?1256725103 (accessed 12 February 2010).

Bell, D. (1979) *Social Science since the Second World War*, New Brunswick, NJ: Transaction Books.

Braye, S. and Preston-Shoot, M. (2005) 'Emerging from out of the shadows? Service user and carer involvement in systematic reviews', *Evidence & Policy,* 1(2): 173–93.

British Academy (2008) *Punching our Weight: the humanities and social sciences in public policy making.* Online. Available: http://www.sis.ac.uk/Wilson_Report.pdf (accessed 1 October 2009).

British Educational Research Association (BERA) (2008) *The 2008 BERA Charter for Research Staff.* Online. Available: http://www.bera.ac.uk/files/guidelines/bera-charter.pdf (accessed 12 November 2009).

Brown, A. (1992) 'Design experiments: theoretical and methodological challenges in creating complex interventions in classroom settings', *Journal of the Learning Sciences,* 2(2): 141–78.

Brown, C. (2009) 'Effective research communication and its role in the development of evidence based policy-making. A case study of the Training and Development Agency for Schools', MA dissertation, Institute of Education, University of London.

Cabinet Office Strategy Unit (2009) *Power in People's Hands: learning from the world's best public services.* Online. Available: http://www.cabinetoffice.gov.uk/media/224869/world-class.pdf (accessed 3 February 2010).

Campbell, R. J., Robinson, W., Neelands, J., Hewston, R. and Mazzoli, L. (2007) 'Personalised learning: ambiguities in theory and practice', *British Journal of Educational Studies,* 55(2): 135–54.

Campbell, S., Benita, S., Coates, E., Davies, P. and Penn, G. (2007) *Analysis for Policy: evidence-based policy in practice.* Online. Available: http://www.gsr.gov.uk/downloads/resources/pu256_160407.pdf (accessed 12 May 2010).

Canadian Health Services Research Foundation (CHSRF) (n.d.) 'Policy on open access to research outputs'. Online. Available: http://www.chsrf.ca/AboutUs/funding_granting/policy.aspx (accessed 7 January 2011).

Carlile, P. (2004) 'Transferring, translating and transforming: an integrative framework for managing knowledge across boundaries', *Organization Science,* 15(5): 555–68.

Chaiklin, S. (1993) 'Understanding the social scientific practice of *Understanding practice*', in S. Chaiklin and J. Lave (eds) *Understanding Practice: perspectives on activity and context*, Cambridge: Cambridge University Press.

Chapman, J. (2002) *System Failure: why governments must learn to think differently,* London: Demos.

Children's Workforce Development Council (CWDC) (2004) *National Occupational Standards in Children's Care, Learning and Development.*

Online. Available: http://www.cwdcouncil.org.uk/nos/ccld-level-3 (accessed 1 June 2010).

Cobb, P., Confrey, J., diSessa, A., Lehrer, R. and Schauble, L. (2003) 'Design experiments in educational research', *Educational Researcher*, 32(1): 9–13.

Collins, A. (1992) 'Towards a design science of education', in E. Scanlon and T. O'Shea (eds) *New Directions in Educational Technology*, Berlin: Springer-Verlag.

Collins, A., Joseph, D. and Bielaczyc, K. (2004) 'Design research: theoretical and methodological issues', *Journal of the Learning Sciences*, 13(1): 15–42.

Commission on the Social Sciences (2003) *Great Expectations: the social sciences in Britain*. Online. Available: http://www.acss.org.uk/docs/GtExpectations.pdf (accessed 2 December 2010).

Concordat to Support the Career Development of Researchers (2008) *Concordat to Support the Career Development of Researchers*. Online. Available: http://www.researchconcordat.ac.uk/documents/concordat.pdf (accessed 1 December 2009).

Connell, J. and Kubisch, A. (1998) *Applying a Theory of Change Approach to the Evaluation of Comprehensive Community Initiatives: progress, prospects, and problems,* Aspen CO: Aspen Institute.

Cooper, A. and Levin, B. (2010) 'Some Canadian contributions to understanding knowledge mobilisation', *Evidence and Policy* (in press).

Cooper, A., Levin, B. and Campbell, C. (2009) 'The growing (but still limited) importance of evidence in education policy and practice', *Journal of Educational Change*, 10(2–3): 159–71.

Davies, H. T. O., Nutley, S. M. and Smith, P. C. (1999) 'What works? The role of evidence in public sector policy and practice', *Public Money and Management,* 19: 3–5.

Davies, H. T. O., Nutley, S. and Walter, I. (2008) 'Why "knowledge transfer" is misconceived for applied social research', *Journal of Health Services Research and Policy*, 13(3): 188–90.

Department for Children, Schools and Families (DCSF) (2008) *Analysis and Evidence Strategy*. Online. Available: http://www.dcsf.gov.uk/research/data/general/Analysis%20and%20Evidence%20Strategy%20(AES-2008).pdf (accessed 5 March 2010).

Department of Education, Training and Youth Affairs (DETYA) (2000) *The Impact of Educational Research*. Online. Available: http://www.detya.gov.au/highered/respubs/impact/overview.htm (accessed 3 June 2010).

Dowse, L. (2009) '"It's like being in a zoo": researching with people with intellectual disability', *Journal of Research in Special Educational Needs*, 9(3): 141–53.

Economic and Social Research Council (ESRC) (2009a) *Taking Stock: a summary of ESRC's work to evaluate the impact of research on policy*

and practice. Online. Available: http://www.esrc.ac.uk/ESRCInfoCentre/Images/taking_stock_tcm6–30940.pdf (accessed 10 November 2009).
— (2009b) *ESRC Research Funding Guide Post fEC.* Online. Available: http://www.esrcsocietytoday.ac.uk/ESRCInfoCentre/Images/ESRC_Research_Funding_Guide_tcm6–9734.pdf (accessed 24 October 2009).
— (2009c) *ESRC Postgraduate Training and Development Guidelines 2009.* Online. Available: http://www.esrcsocietytoday.ac.uk/ESRCInfoCentre/Images/Postgraduate%20Training%20and%20Development%20Guidelines_tcm6–33067.pdf (accessed 25 November 2009).
— (2010a) 'How to write a good application', *ESRC Society Today.* Online. Available: http://www.esrc.ac.uk/ESRCInfoCentre/Support/research_award_holders/FAQs2/index1.aspx (accessed 8 November 2010).
— (2010b) 'Knowledge exchange opportunites'. Online. Available: http://www.esrcsocietytoday.ac.uk/ESRCInfoCentre/KnowledgeExch/index.aspx (accessed 15 December 2010).
Edwards, A. (2001) 'Researching pedagogy: a sociocultural agenda', *Pedagogy, Culture and Society,* 9(2): 161–86.
— (2002) 'Responsible research: ways of being a researcher', *British Educational Research Journal,* 28(2): 157–68.
— (2010) *Being an Expert Professional Practitioner: the relational turn in expertise,* Dordrecht: Springer.
Edwards, A., Sebba, J. and Rickinson, M. (2006b) 'Working with users in educational research: some implications for research capacity building', *Building Research Capacity,* (11): 1–4.
— (2007) 'Working with users: the implications for educational research', *British Educational Research Journal,* 33(5): 647–61.
— (2009b) *Making a Difference: collaborating with users to develop educational research; TLRP Research Briefing No 76.* Online. Available: http://www.tlrp.org/pub/documents/EdwardsA%20RB76%20Final.pdf (accessed 12 February 2010).
Edwards, A., Lunt, I. and Stamou, E. (2010) 'Inter-professional work and expertise: new roles at the boundaries of schools', *British Educational Research Journal,* 36(1): 27–45.
Edwards, A., Barnes, M., Plewis, I. and Morris, K. (2006a) *Working to prevent the Social Exclusion of Children and Young People: Final Lessons from the National Evaluation of the Children's Fund.* DfES Research Report 734, London: DfES.
Edwards, A., Daniels, H., Gallagher, T., Leadbetter, J. and Warmington, P. (2009a) *Improving Inter-professional Collaborations: multi-agency working for children's wellbeing,* London: Routledge.
Ellis, V. (2010) 'Studying the process of change: the double stimulation strategy in teacher education research', in V. Ellis, A. Edwards and P. Smagorinsky (eds) *Cultural-historical Perspectives on Teacher Education and Development,* London: Routledge.

Engeström, Y. (1999) 'Activity theory and individual and social transformation', in Y. Engeström, R. Miettinen and R.-L. Punamäki (eds) *Perspectives on Activity Theory*, Cambridge: Cambridge University Press.

— (2007) 'Putting activity theory to work: the change laboratory as an application of double stimulation', in H. Daniels, M. Cole and J. V. Wertsch (eds) *The Cambridge Companion to Vygotsky*, Cambridge: Cambridge University Press.

— (2008) *From Teams to Knots: activity theoretical studies of collaboration and learning at work*, Cambridge: Cambridge University Press.

Evetts, J. (2009) 'New professionalism and new public management: changes continuities and consequences', *Comparative Sociology*, 8: 247–66.

Facts in Education (2010) 'The facts on school choice and decentralization', *Facts in Education*, 7 April. Online. Available at http://factsineducation. blogspot.com/2010/04/facts-on-school-choice-and.html (accessed 2 December 2010).

Fielding, M. (2001) 'Students as radical agents of change', *Journal of Educational Change*, 2: 123–41.

Fielding, M. and Bragg, S. (2003) *Students as Researchers: making a difference*, Cambridge: Pearson.

Flyvbjerg, B. (2001) *Making Social Science Matter*, Cambridge: Cambridge University Press.

Foster, M., Harris, J., Jackson, K., Morgan, H. and Glendinning, C. (2006) 'Personalised social care for adults with disabilities: a problematic concept for frontline practice', *Health and Social Care in the Community*, 14(2): 125–35.

Foster, P. and Hammersley, M. (1998) 'A review of reviews: structure and function in reviews of educational research', *British Educational Research Journal*, 24(5): 609–28.

Furlong, J. and Oancea, A. (2005) *Assessing Quality in Applied and Practice-based Educational Research: a framework for discussion*, Oxford: Oxford University Department of Educational Studies.

Furlong, J. and Salisbury, J. (2005) 'Best practice research scholarships: an evaluation', *Research Papers in Education*, 20(1): 45–83.

Garcia, J., Sinclair, J., Dickson, K., Thomas, J., Brunton, J., Tidd, M. and the PSHE Review Group (2006) *Conflict Resolution, Peer Mediation and Young People's Relationships: review conducted by the Personal, Social and Health Education (PSHE) school-based Review Group. Technical report.* Online. Available: http://eppi.ioe.ac.uk/cms/LinkClick.aspx?file ticket=NZ7TOKwLxp4%3d&tabid=708&mid=1621&language=en-US (accessed 3 June 2010).

Gardiner, P. (1988) *Kierkegaard*, Oxford: Oxford University Press.

Gibbons, M. (1999) 'Science's new social contract', *Nature* 402(6761 Suppl): C81–C84.

Gibbons, M., Limoges, C., Nowotny, H., Schwartzman, S., Scott, P. and Trow, M. (1994) *The New Production of Knowledge,* London: Sage.

Goldacre, B. (2009) 'Influence from the sun and moon', Bad Science Series, *Guardian*, 31 October.

Gough, P. R., Lajoie, J., Shlonsky, A. and Trocmé, N. (2009) 'Journal Watch: an inter-university collaborative learning partnership', *Social Work Education*, 29(1): 18–26.

Haas, E. (2007) 'False equivalency: think tank references on education in the news media', *Peabody Journal of Education*, 82(1): 63–102.

Hargreaves, D. (1998) 'A new partnership of stakeholders and a national strategy for research in education', in J. Rudduck and D. McIntyre (eds) *Challenges for Educational Research*, London: Paul Chapman.

Harlen, W. (1977) 'A stronger teacher role in curriculum development?', *Curriculum Studies* 9(1): 21–9.

Higher Education Funding Council for England (HEFCE) (2009) *Research Excellence Framework: impact pilot exercise*. Online. Available: http://www.hefce.ac.uk/research/ref/impact (accessed 10 February 2010).

— (2010) *Annex A: initial decisions on the Research Excellence Framework*. Online. Available: http://www.hefce.ac.uk/pubs/circlets/2010/cl04_10/cl04_10a.pdf (accessed 5 June 2010).

Hillage, J., Pearson, R., Anderson, A. and Tamkin, P. (1998) *Excellence in Research on Schools*, DfEE Research Report 74, London: DfEE.

HM Government (2009) *Building Britain's Future*, CM7654. Norwich: The Stationery Office.

Hodkinson, P. and Smith, J. K. (2004) 'The relationship between research, policy and practice', in G. Thomas, and R. Pring (eds) *Evidence-based Practice in Education*, Maidenhead: Open University Press.

Huberman, M. (1987) 'Steps towards an integrated model of research utilization', *Knowledge*, 8: 586–611.

— (1990) 'Linkage between researchers and practitioners: a qualitative study', *American Educational Research Journal*, 27: 363–91.

— (1993) 'Linking the practitioner and research communities for school improvement', *School Effectiveness and School Improvement*, 4(1): 1–16.

Innvaer, S., Vist, G., Trommald, M. and Oxman, A. (2002) 'Health policy-makers' perceptions of their use of evidence: a systematic review', *Journal of Health Services Research and Policy*, 7(4): 239–44.

Jacklin, A., Robinson, C., O'Meara, L. and Harris, A. (2007) *Improving the Experiences of Disabled Students in Higher Education*, York: Higher Education Academy.

Kahn, P., Wareham, T. and Young, R. (2006) 'Evaluation of a collaborative practitioner review methodology developed for a review of the effectiveness of reflective practices in programmes for new academic staff in universities', paper presented at British Educational Research Association Annual Conference, University of Warwick, September 2006.

Kennedy, M. (1997) 'The connection between research and practice', *Educational Researcher,* 26(7): 9–17.

Kirst, M. W. (2000) 'Bridging education research and education policymaking', *Oxford Review of Education*, 26(4): 379–91.

Knight, L. and Pettigrew, A. (2007) 'Explaining process and performance in the co-production of knowledge: a comparative analysis of collaborative research projects', paper presented at the Organization Studies Third Summer Workshop, Crete, Greece, June 2007.

Knorr Cetina, K. (1999) *Epistemic Cultures: how sciences make knowledge*, Cambridge, MA: Harvard University Press.

Knott, J. H. and Weissert, C. S. (1996) *Linking Ideas to Policy: what can be learned from foundations' efforts to inform health policymakers*, East Lansing, MI: Institute for Public Policy and Social Research.

Landry, R., Amara, N. and Lamari, M. (2001) 'Utilization of social science research knowledge in Canada', *Research Policy*, 30: 333–49.

— (2003) 'The extent and determinants of utilization of university research in government agencies', *Public Administration Review*, 63(2): 192–205.

Lavis, J. N., McLeod, C. B. and Gildiner, A. (2003) 'Measuring the impact of health research', *Journal of Health Services Research and Policy*, 8: 165–70.

Leadbeater, C. (2004) *Learning about Personalisation: how can we put the learner at the heart of the education system?*, London: Demos.

Lencucha, R., Kothari, A. and Hamel, N. (2010) 'Extending collaborations for knowledge translation: lessons from the community based participatory research literature', *Evidence & Policy,* 6(1): 61–75.

Levin, B. (2004a) 'Media-government relations in education', *Journal of Education Policy,* 19(3): 271–83.

— (2004b) 'Making research in education to matter more', *Education and Policy Archives,* 12(56): 1–22.

— (2008) 'Thinking about knowledge mobilisation', paper prepared for an invitational symposium sponsored by the Canadian Council on Learning and the Social Sciences and the Humanities Research Council of Canada, May 2008.

Lomas, J. (1993) 'Diffusion, dissemination and implementation: who should do what?', *Annals of the New York Academy of Sciences*, 703: 226–35.

Lomas, J., Culyer, T., McCutcheon, C., McAuley, L. and Law, S. (2005) *Conceptualizing and Combining Evidence for Health System Guidance.* Online. Available: http://www.chsrf.ca/other_documents/pdf/evidence_e.pdf (accessed 3 March 2010).

Lundvall, B.-Å. (1996) 'The social dimension of the learning economy', *DRUID Working Paper* No. 96–1.

— (2000) 'The learning economy: some implications for the knowledge base of health and education systems', in OECD/CERI (eds) *Knowledge Management in the Learning Society*, Paris: OECD/CERI.

McIntyre, D. (1998) 'The usefulness of educational research: an agenda for consideration and action', in J. Rudduck and D. McIntyre (eds) *Challenges for Educational Research*, London: Paul Chapman.

McLaughlin, C. and Black-Hawkins, K., with Townsend, A. (2005) *Practitioner Research and Enquiry within Networked Learning Communities*, Nottingham: NCSL.

McNutt, K. and Marchildon, G. (2009) 'Think tanks and the web: measuring visibility and influence', *Canadian Public Policy*, 35(2): 219–36.

Martinez, N. R. and Campbell, D. (2007) 'Using knowledge brokering to promote evidence-based policy-making', *Bulletin of the World Health Organization*, 85(5): 325–420.

Miliband, D. (2004) *Personalised Learning: building a new relationship with schools*, speech to North of England Education Conference, Belfast 8 January. Online. Available http://publications.teachernet.gov.uk/eOrderingDownload/personalised-learning.pdf (accessed 4 May 2010).

Millar, R. (2002) 'Towards evidence-based practice in science education', *School Science Review*, 84 (307): 19–20.

Mitchell, F., Lunt, N. and Shaw, I. (2010) 'Practitioner research in social work: a knowledge review', *Evidence & Policy,* 6: 7–31.

Mollas-Gallart, J., Tang, P. and Morros, S. (2000) 'Assessing the non-academic impact of grant-funded socio-economic research: results from a pilot study', *Research Evaluation*, 9(3): 171–82.

Morris, A., Percy-Smith, J. and Rickinson, M. (2007) *Practitioners and Evidence: designing research and development to influence practice*, Reading: CfBT.

Mulgan, G. (2005) 'Government, knowledge and the business of policy making: the potential and limits of evidence-based policy', *Evidence & Policy,* 1(2): 215–26.

Munn, P., Ozga, J., Raffe, D., Simpson, M., Allan, J., Boreham, N., Johnstone, R., Morris, B., Bryce, T., Christie, D., Humes, W. and Livingston, K. (2003) *A Collaborative Proposal for a National Programme of Infrastructure Development and Research.* Online. Available: http://www.aers.org.uk/aers/index.php?option=com_content&task=view&id=12&Itemid=26 (accessed 15 November 2009).

Nissen, M. (2009) 'Objectification and prototype', *Qualitative Research in Psychology,* 6(1): 67–87.

Nonaki, I. and Takeuchi, H. (1995) *The Knowledge Creating Company*, Oxford: Oxford University Press.

Nowotny, H. (2000) 'Transgressive competence: the narrative of expertise', *European Journal of Social Theory*, 3(1): 5–21.

— (2003) 'Dilemma of expertise', *Science and Public Policy*, 30(3): 151–6.

Nuffield Foundation (2010) *2010 Guide to Grants for Research and Innovation.* Online. Available: http://www.nuffieldfoundation.org/sites/default/files/files/Grants%20for%20research%20and%20innovation%20%20-%20complete%20guide%202010v13_09_10(3).pdf (accessed 12 March 2010).

Nutley, S. M. (2005) 'Models of the research-policy relationship', paper presented at Seminar 2 of the User Engagement Thematic Seminar Series, Institute of Education, University of London, London, 24 May 2005.

Nutley, S. M., Walter, I. and Davies, H. (2007) *Using Evidence: how research can inform public services*, Bristol: The Policy Press.

Oakley, A. (2000) *Experiments in Knowing: gender and method in the social sciences*, Cambridge: Polity Press.

Oancea, A. (2005) 'Criticisms of educational research', *British Educational Research Journal*, 31(2): 157–83.

Ontario Ministry of Education (2010) *Research and Evaluation Strategy*, Ontario: Queen's Printer for Ontario. Online. Available: www.edu.gov.on.ca/eng/research/research.pdf (accessed 15 December 2010).

Organisation for Economic Co-operation and Development (OECD) Centre of Educational Research and Innovation (CERI) (2002) *Educational Research and Development in England: Examiners' Report*, Paris: OECD/CERI.

— (2007) *Evidence in Education: linking research and policy*, Paris: OECD/CERI.

Pawson, R. (2003) *Assessing the Quality of Evidence in Evidence-based Policy: why, how and when?* Online. Available: http://www.ccsr.ac.uk/methods/publications/Pawson.pdf (accessed 3 June 2010).

Phipps, D. J. and Shapson, S. (2009) 'Knowledge mobilisation builds local research collaborations for social innovation', *Evidence & Policy*, 5(3): 211–27.

Pollard, A. (2004) 'The SERA lecture 2003: what is and what might be? TLRP strategies and the development of educational research', *Scottish Educational Review,* 36(1): 11–21.

Prost, A. (2001) *Pour un programme stratégique de recherche en education. Report to the ministers d'Education nationale et de la Recherche*, Paris: Ministere de l'Education nationale.

Punch, S. (2002) 'Research with children: the same or different from research with adults', *Childhood*, 9(3): 321–41.

Research Assessment Exercise (RAE) (2008) *Sub-panel 45 Education Subject Overview Report*. Online. Available: http://www.sfre.ac.uk/wp-content/uploads/2009/01/uoa45-education.pdf (accessed 6 October 2009).

ResearchImpact (2008) 'ResearchImpact hosts Canada's first virtual Aboriginal Policy Research Forum', *ResearchImpact*. Online. Available: www.researchimpact.ca/kmbinaction/aboriginal/index.html (accessed 1 December 2010).

Rich, A. (2004) *Think Tanks, Public Policy and the Politics of Expertise*, Cambridge: Cambridge University Press.

Rickinson, M., Walker, M. and Rudd, P. (2005) *Mid-term Review of the ESRC Teaching and Learning Research Programme*. Online. Available: http://www.tlrp.org/manage/documents/NFER_Final_TLRP_Report_March_2005.pdf (10 October 2009).

Rigby, E. (2005) 'Linking research and policy on Capitol Hill', *Evidence and Policy*, 1: 195–213.

Royal College of General Practitioners (2006) *Curriculum Statement*

3.6. Online. Available: http://www.gmc-uk.org/3_6_Research_01. pdf_30450718.pdf (accessed 31 May 2010).

Rudduck, J. and McIntyre, D. (eds) (1998) *Challenges for Educational Research*, London: Paul Chapman.

Rudduck, J., Brown, N. and Hendy, L. (2005) 'Personalised learning: the East Sussex project', paper presented at the DfES Conference, November 2005.

Ruthven, K., Laborde, C., Leach, J. and Tiberghien, A. (2009) 'Design tools in didactical research: instrumenting the epistemological and cognitive aspects of the design of teaching sequences', *Educational Researcher*, 38(5): 329–42.

Saunders, L. (ed.) (2007a) *Educational Research and Policy-making*, London: Routledge.

— (2007b) 'Editor's introduction', in L. Saunders (ed.) *Educational Research and Policy-making*, London: Routledge.

Sebba, J. (2007) 'Enhancing impact on policy-making through increasing user engagement in research', in L. Saunders (ed.) *Educational Research and Policy-making,* London: Routledge.

Sebba, J. and Robinson, C. (2010) *Evaluation of UNICEF UK's Rights Respecting Schools Award (RRSA)*, London: UNICEF.

Seely Brown, J. and Duguid, P. (2002) *The Social Life of Information*, Boston, MA: Harvard Business School Press.

Shakespeare, T. (1993) 'Disabled people's self-organisation: a new social movement?', *Disability, Handicap and Society*, 8(3): 249–64.

— (2006) *Disability Rights and Wrongs*, London: Routledge.

Sharland, E. and Taylor, I. (2006) 'Social care research: a suitable case for systematic review?', *Evidence & Policy*, 2: 503–23.

Shavelson, R. J. and Towne, L. (2002) *Scientific Research in Education*, Washington DC: National Academy Press.

Slavin, R. (2002) 'Evidence-based education policies: transforming educational practice and research', *Educational Researcher*, 31(7): 15–21.

Somekh, B. (2007) 'The interplay between policy and research in relation to ICT in education in the UK: issues from twenty years of programme evaluation', in L. Saunders (ed.) *Educational Research and Policy-making*, London: Routledge.

Stehr, N. (1994) *Knowledge Societies*, London: Sage.

Sullivan, H., Barnes, M. and Matka, E. (2002) 'Building collaborative capacity through "Theories of Change": early lessons from the evaluation of Health Action Zones in England', *Evaluation,* 8(2): 205–26.

Sutherland, R., John, P. and Robertson, S. (2007) *Improving Learning with ICT*, London: Routledge.

Sylva, K., Taggart, B., Melhuish, E., Sammons, P. and Siraj-Blatchford, I. (2007) 'Changing models of research to inform educational policy', *Research Papers in Education*, 22(2): 155–68.

Taylor, C., Connolly, M., Power, S. and Rees, G. (2007) *Formative Evaluation of the Applied Educational Research Scheme (AERS)*. Online. Available:

http://www.scotland.gov.uk/Resource/Doc/208243/0055238.pdf (accessed 12 May 2010).

Tetroe, J. M., Graham, I. D, Foy, R., Robinson, N., Eccles, M. P., Wensing, M., Durieux, P., Légaré, F., Palmhøj Nielson, C., Adily, A., Ward, J. E., Porter, C., Shea, B. and Grimshaw, J. M. (2008) 'Health research funding agencies' support and promotion of knowledge translation: an international study', *Milbank Quarterly*, 86(1): 125–55.

TLRP (2006) *Using Computers to Enhance Learning: integrating ICT into everyday classroom practices*, TLRP Research Briefing No. 19. Online. Available: http://www.tlrp.org/pub/documents/Sutherland_RB_19.pdf (accessed 31 May 2010).

— (n.d.) 'Towards evidence based practice in science education 2000–2003'. Online. Available: http://www.tlrp.org/proj/phase1/phase1bsept.html (accessed 15 December 2010).

Thomson, P. and Gunter, H. (2006) 'From "consulting pupils" to "pupils as researchers": a situated case narrative', *British Educational Research Journal*, 32(6): 839–56.

Training and Development Agency for Schools (TDA) (2007) *Professional Standards for Teachers*. Online. Available: http://www.tda.gov.uk/upload/resources/pdf/s/standards_a4.pdf (accessed 29 June 10).

van den Acker, J., Gravemeijer, K., McKenney, S. and Nieveen, N. (2006) *Educational Design Research*, London: Routledge.

Walter, I., Nutley, S., Percy-Smith, J., McNeish, D. and Frost, S. (2004) *Improving the Use of Social Care Research*, SCIE Knowledge Review 7. Online. Available: http://www.scie.org.uk/publications/knowledge reviews/kr07.pdf (accessed 31 May 2010).

Ward, V., House, A. and Hamer, S. (2009) 'Knowledge brokering: the missing link in the evidence to action chain?', *Evidence & Policy,* 5: 267–79.

Webb, S. (2002) 'Evidence-based practice and decision analysis in social work: an implementation model', *Journal of Social Work*, 2(1): 45–64.

— (2008) 'Modelling service user participation in social care', *Journal of Social Work*, 8: 269–90.

Weiss, C. H. (1979) 'The many meanings of research utilization', *Public Administration Review*, 39(5): 426–31.

— (1980) 'Knowledge creep and decision accretion', *Science Communication*, 1: 381–404.

Whitty, G. (2002) *Making Sense of Education Policy*, London: Paul Chapman.

Willinsky, J. (2005) 'Scientific research in a democratic culture: or what is social science for?', *Teachers College Record,* 107(1): 38–51.

Winch, C. (2001) 'Accountability and relevance in educational research', *Journal of Philosophy of Education,* 35: 443–59.

Winter, M., Smith, C., Morris, P. and Cicmil, S. (2006) 'Directions for future research in project management: the main findings of a UK government-funded research network', *International Journal of Project Management*, 24: 638–49.

Index